THE SUNDAY TIMES
Holidays Online

THE SUNDAY TIMES
Holidays Online

Matthew Wall

HarperCollins*Publishers*

Matthew Wall is a freelance journalist and TV researcher/
producer best-known for his weekly *Web Wise* internet
column in *The Sunday Times*. He also writes internet features
for the paper's Doors section and has written several internet
reports for business. He also advises companies on web
design and strategy.

HarperCollins Publishers
77–85 Fulham Palace Road
Hammersmith
London W6 8JB

fireand**water**.com
Visit the book lover's website

First published 2001

Reprint 10 9 8 7 6 5 4 3 2 1 0

ISBN 0 00 710240-2

Designer: Sylvie Rabbe
Editor: Sarah Barlow

Designed, edited and typeset by Book Creation Services Ltd.

Printed in Great Britain by Omnia Books Ltd, Glasgow G64.

Acknowledgments

I would like to thank my wife, Wendy, for her patience and encouragement during the writing of this book. She kept the coffee flowing and confiscated my games disks – essential interventions for which I am truly grateful. I would also like to thank Christopher Riches at HarperCollins for his flexible interpretation of the word deadline.

Matthew Wall

March 2001

Contents

Introduction

Welcome

Welcome to *The Sunday Times Guide to Holidays Online*. Here you'll find heaps of useful websites, tips and advice to help you plan and book your journey or holiday. If you want to get to work on time or go on a white-water rafting adventure holiday, this book has something for you.

The guide is aimed at people who are already familiar with web basics. If you're new to the whole experience, you may prefer to read *The Sunday Times Guide to the Internet* first.

Travel online is booming

Travel online is one of the fastest-growing areas of e-commerce. Maybe it's because none of us can resist the lure of sunnier climes, especially when the web seems to bring them just a few mouse-clicks away. In February 2001, researcher NOP reported that British online shoppers now spend more on holidays and travel than on anything else they buy over the web.

NOP estimates that around 480,000 people shopped for holidays and travel online in the four weeks leading up to Christmas 2000, spending an average of £420 a head, well ahead of the 335,000 online grocery shoppers who spent an average of £113 each. This level of growth is likely to continue as interest in travel increases and intense competition amongst travel operators continues to bring prices down.

Why use the web?

The web and travel go very well together. For a start, getting from A to B, often via C, is a very complicated business. There's just so much information to deal with when you travel, from timetables and route planning to hotel

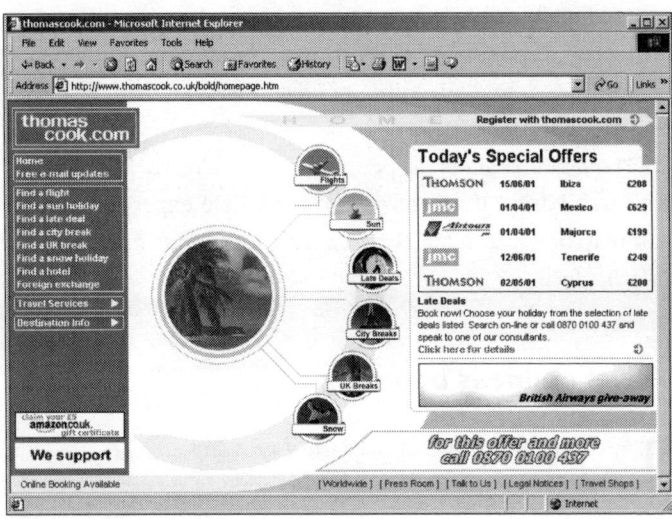

There is a no more efficient and economical way for a travel company, big or small, to advertise all of its products in one place than on the internet. In addition, the company is instantly in touch with, and selling holidays to customers all over the world.

addresses and foreign currency. Arranging all these separate components of a journey can be a headache at the best of times, especially when several of the elements are subject to sudden change.

Luckily the web is particularly good at sifting and sorting vast quantities of data and disseminating it to the masses from one central, convenient place. Information can be updated very quickly online, making the web perfect for accessing the latest deals on flights and holidays, and news about disruptions to the rail network.

Holiday companies can advertise their wares more efficiently through a single website than via thousands of very expensive brochures. And online travel sites can aggregate all the competing holidays and trips into one place where we can search and compare all that's on offer. It's just so much more efficient.

Travel portals, such as Ebookers (www.ebookers.com) are an invaluable source of reference for the best price on flights, holidays, accommodation and other travel related services. Their links with other websites will immediately direct you to the right product for you.

This ability of the web to be bang up-to-date means that flexible travellers can pick up some fantastic last-minute bargains online. Travel operators don't mind because they can sell excess capacity more efficiently this way. It's better to get £5 for a filled seat on a plane than to have that seat empty. And technology has also helped introduce innovations such as online auctions, where people bid against each other, and reverse auctions, where people can stipulate the price they are willing to pay and see if the travel company accepts.

In short, the web has provided an extremely useful platform for the travel industry to distribute its products and services far more efficiently than before.

Is the web always cheaper?

Unfortunately, no. Although there are plenty of bargains to be found online and comparing and contrasting prices has never been easier, it's still a mistake to assume that prices will always be lower than you can find in your local travel agent or bucket shop. A high-street agent may have a strong relationship with a particular holiday company or airline and be in a position to offer even better prices

WARNING

Although there are plenty of bargains to be found online, don't assume that prices will always be lower than in your local travel agent or bucket shop.

So if you have the time and the inclination, a trip to the high street is still sometimes a good idea, if only to convince you that you're getting a good deal online. But the web is fantastic as a research and booking tool, saving you hours of time and trouble. That in itself can save you money. And in the broader scheme of things, by making it easier to distribute timely information and improve booking procedures, the web is helping travel companies to squeeze costs out of the system.

There are just so many holidays and travel companies around and not all of them have a web presence. So although the web is having a profound effect on the travel industry, it's unlikely to put high-street travel agents out of business overnight. Lots of people still like to talk to someone to discuss their travel requirements, and pop into an agent on impulse when they're walking down the street. Also, people still like the idea of having a real person to complain to or ask advice of if things go wrong.

Is it safe?

There are a lot of myths spread about the safety of the web. Stories of hackers stealing credit card details and running up huge bills do nothing to help matters. But most of these fears are unfounded. Yes, credit card details have occasionally been stolen, but the cardholders haven't

> **TIP**
>
> *When you buy online you have just as many consumer rights as you do when you buy through any other medium.*

lost out because it usually wasn't their fault. It's the online retailers and card issuers that bear the brunt of online fraud. And anyway, this kind of hacking is still pretty rare, despite the scare stories.

Ordering tickets and paying online using plastic cards is actually safer than ordering over the phone. When you send sensitive data, such as credit card details, across the web, they are encrypted – jumbled up using a complicated mathematical formula – before they go. This makes it virtually impossible for anyone to intercept and decipher them while they are in transit. Although there are still residual concerns about transacting online, the fact that people are spending more, and doing so more frequently, shows that the safety message is finally getting across.

Of more concern is the probity and integrity of the company you're dealing with online. There are good and bad companies in the high street and the same goes for the web. By using a little common sense and following our guidelines (*see* **Safe surfing**, *page 129*), you can book tickets and buy holidays online with confidence.

How to use this guide

This guide is organised along functional lines. It's not intended to be read all the way through. Simply go to the section that is relevant to the type of travel or holiday that interests you. Broadly speaking, there are four sections: research and planning; booking component parts, such as flights, accommodation and car rental; researching and buying all-in-one holidays; and protecting yourself and knowing your rights.

> **TIP**
>
> *Ordering tickets and paying online using plastic cards is actually safer than ordering over the phone.*

The difficulty from an organisational point of view is that many of the websites reviewed attempt to be all things to everyone, and so there is often some overlap between sections. If readers have any suggestions for new sections to include, we'd be only too happy to hear from you!

Before launching yourself on the web, decide what kind of holiday you are looking for. Is it a weekend break, a luxury cruise, or a week's skiing in the Alps? Do you mind a package deal or do you want to structure the holiday for yourself? Can you leave at the drop of a hat in return for a rock-bottom price, or are you prepared to pay more to have arrangements exactly as you want them? The answers to these questions will help you choose the relevant section of the guide.

Most travel-related companies have a website these days, from airlines to car rental firms, hotel chains to travel agents. There are hundreds and hundreds of sites out there and this guide certainly doesn't review them all. We've simply taken a cross section of the best to make your life as easy as possible.

Chapter 2

Planning Your Trip or Holiday

Introduction

I think it was some ancient Greek who said that if you plan any endeavour properly you're already halfway there before you even begin. This is true when it comes to travel. How many of us arrive at our holiday destination completely stressed out simply because of the difficulties associated with organising the trip in the first place? We often feel we need another holiday to recover. In this chapter, we've collected all the resources you could possibly require to help you plan and prepare for your journey. From timetables to travel guides, maps to health information, almost everything you need is online these days. Forewarned is forearmed

> **TIP**
>
> *Spend some time browsing on the net when planning a trip. There's a wealth of information out there about how to get to your destination and what to expect when you arrive.*

they say, so, in the words of Lord Baden-Powell, be prepared!

Timetables and ticket booking services

General

UK Public Transport Information (www.pti.org.uk)

A useful all-in-one site covering most forms of public transport, including air, rail, ferry, coach and bus services. It confidently boasts: 'If it's not here it's not on the web.' The comprehensiveness of the site means that it is only updated weekly though, so don't rely on it for the very latest news.

UK Rail Information

Railtrack (www.railtrack.com)

Railtrack's site declares 'we're the heart of the railway', inciting inevitable jokes about cardiac arrests. You can normally interrogate national timetables on the Railtrack site, but it has not always been to keep up to date with

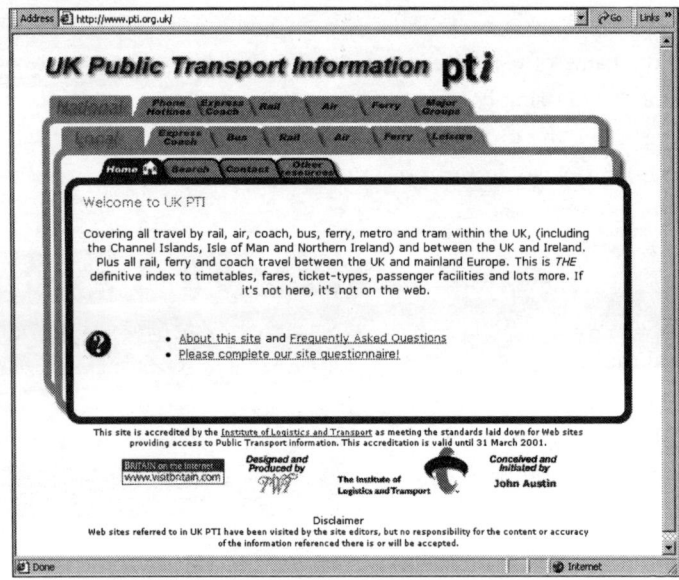

The UK Public Transport Information website (www.pti.org.uk) is a comprehensive guide to all forms of transport in the United Kingdom.

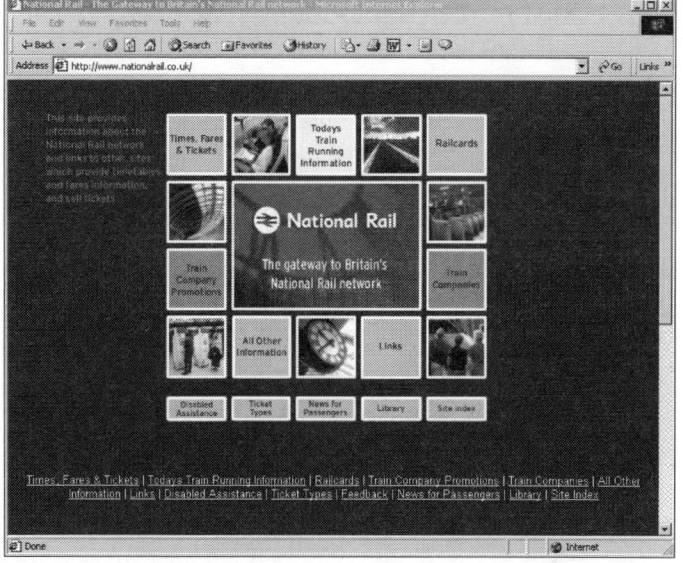

The National Rail portal (www.nationalrail.co.uk) provides up-to-date information on Britain's railway network as well as providing links to individual rail companies.

engineering work, so you may have to look elsewhere. You can find out the latest news via various links on the Railtrack site. For example, if you want to know which lines are still subject to speed restrictions you can look at a colour-coded map of the area relevant to you.

National Rail (www.nationalrail.co.uk)

This is an excellent rail information portal. Although it makes grim reading, you can discover out the very latest disruption information from each of the train operating companies. The bulletins are regularly updated, so keep refreshing your browser while you're online.

T I P

Make sure you bookmark the National Rail site because it's a must for travellers by rail.

11

The quality of information is impressively detailed and up-to-date – a far cry from the old days. The rail industry seems at last to have realised that lack of information is one of the most frustrating aspects of rail travel.

The National Rail site also gives contact numbers for all the UK's train operating companies and links through to their websites. To their credit twenty-six rail companies have now set up sites, including such lesser-known train operators as Hull Trains and Island Line, which serves the Isle of Wight. Many of the train operators allow you to book and pay for your tickets online. Virgin Trains, for example, offers a £1 discount if you buy online. Don't get too excited. The rail companies' sites also give details of their special promotions and bargain fares, making them an essential port of call before you plan your journey. In short, rail companies are beginning to behave like airlines, and that is no bad thing.

The Train Line (www.thetrainline.com)

This is the main online rail ticket booking service. Trainline tells you whether seats are available on the train you want and lets you choose the type of ticket. You can pay online using your credit, debit or charge card. But the site doesn't have the latest disruption information, so make sure you check with the National Rail site before booking. Of course, there's no point using Trainline if you're in a hurry because they won't have time to deliver your tickets to you. It's useful for longer-term journey planning and delivery of the tickets is free.

London Transport (www.londontransport.co.uk)

If you want information on what's happening on the London Underground, go to the Transport for London website – the London mayor's attempt to introduce an integrated transport policy for the capital. The site brings together information on buses, the Underground, Docklands Light Railway, taxis and

A website covering every aspect of public transport in London (www.londontransport.co.uk), from maps to fare prices and buying tickets online, was the inspiration of the city's first mayor, Ken Livingstone.

any other mode of transport you can think of. Live transport news is constantly streamed to the site in a 'ticker tape'-style banner. There are maps to help you plan your journey, and you can buy travel cards online, too. It's all unnervingly efficient and helpful.

Docklands Light Railway (www.dlr.co.uk)

Given that the DLR in London has always been at the forefront of new technology with its automated driverless trains, it should come as no surprise that it is trialling several other state-of-the-art services, too. Regular users can arrange to have news bulletins fired to their internet-enabled mobile phones (WAP phones). In February 2001 the company also began testing a real-time on-train news and entertainment system transmitted to the trains by radio signal from base stations.

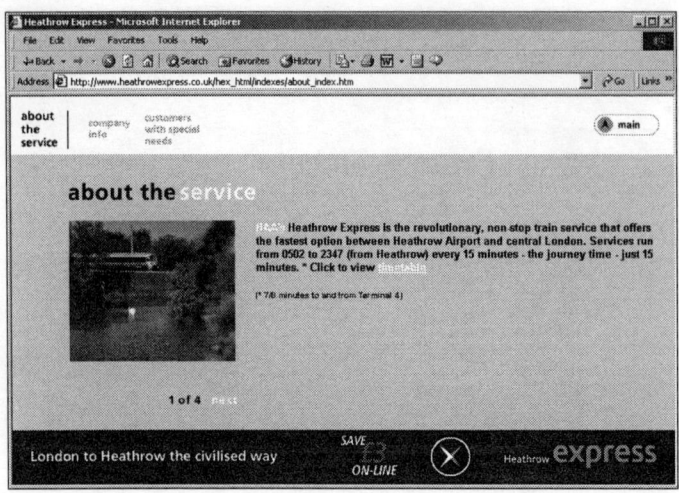

The new direct rail service between Paddington and Heathrow has been quick to advertise its services on the internet (www.heathrowexpress.co.uk), including the incentive of an online fare discount.

Heathrow Express (www.heathrowexpress.co.uk)

If you want to get to Heathrow Airport in a hurry – and you don't mind paying extra for the privilege of avoiding the great unwashed on the Tube – BAA's Heathrow Express lets you book your luggage at Paddington station and guarantees a fast train every fifteen minutes. The site is slickly designed using Flash animation and there's a £3 online booking discount.

International rail information
Eurorailways (www.eurorailways.com)

If you are suffused with the romance of the railways and you fancy crossing countries whilst reclining on a couchette, then this umbrella site is a good place to start planning your epic journey. There's information on how to get single-country and multi-country passes, plus route-planning advice. You can even ring up and talk to a real person.

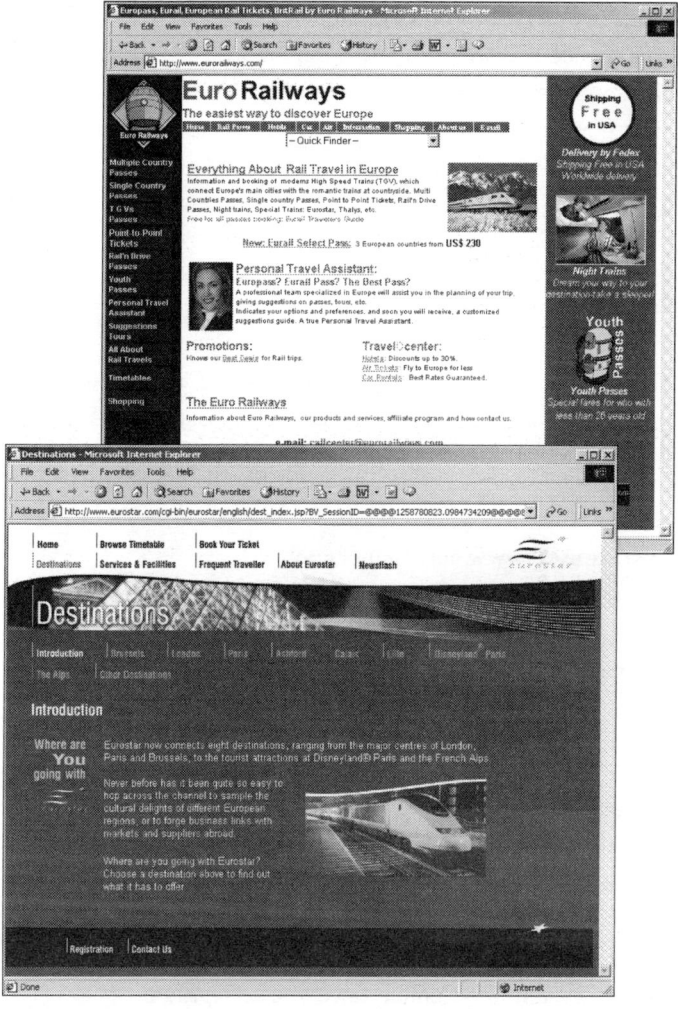

Almost every European country is accessible by rail. Eurostar's easy to use website (bottom, www.eurostar.com) covers information on all its destinations, including timetables and fare prices, while the comprehensive site www.eurorailways.com (top) gives information on routes and fares across the Continent.

Rail Europe (www.raileurope.co.uk)

This service is owned by SNCF, the French national railway, and specialises in European rail travel, concentrating on the most popular countries. Booking is by phone and Rail Europe can also provide accommodation, car rental and insurance services, too.

Eurostar (www.eurostar.com)

Eurostar trains link London, Paris and Brussels. It is a supremely elegant way to travel to the Continent. The website is simple and efficient. You can interrogate the timetable and book your tickets. Don't expect too many frills or special offers, though. Eurostar doesn't have to try that hard.

Eurotunnel (www.eurotunnel.com)

If you like the idea of avoiding nausea, storm delays and rowdy passengers, Le Shuttle is the way to get your car across La Manche in just over half an hour. The Eurotunnel website is neat and well designed and there's a £2 online booking discount into the bargain.

Amtrak (www.amtrak.com)

Amtrak is the main rail operator in the USA, providing all the intercity passenger train services. If you want to see more of the USA without hiring a gas-guzzler, this is the site to head for. You can look at routes and timetables and book online once you've registered on the site.

TrainWeb (www.trainweb.com)

This is a good all-round rail travel site giving lots of links to US and Canadian rail services plus travel tips and route planners. In fact, if you dig deep enough into this labyrinthine site you

This railway portal (www.railserve.com) details train journeys all over the world, including specialist trips – an invaluable site for lovers of rail travel.

can find information on rail travel pretty much anywhere in the world. Also take a look at **RailServe** (**www.railserve.com**) for hundreds of links to the world's railways.

Ferries

P&O Ferries (www.poferries.com)

Just click on the route you want to sail and you are taken to the site of the P&O subsidiary that operates it. Each site is different and has its own special offers. For example, P&O Stena Line offers a new car importing scheme. In each case, you can peruse the timetable and fill in the online booking form. It's all very simple and well designed.

Brittany Ferries (www.brittany-ferries.com)

Ferries from Portsmouth, Poole and Plymouth going to France, Spain and Ireland. Online schedules and booking, but little else.

Hoverspeed (www.hoverspeed.com)

The Hovercraft has finally deflated, so the name is a little misleading, but the company still operates its catamarans and high-speed ferries. The site also makes an attempt to offer other services, such as car importation schemes and short break holidays. Booking is by telephone only.

Ferry Companies of the Web (www.ferrytravel.de)

This catch-all site might not be the prettiest on the web, but it does the job admirably, bringing together links to the world's major ferry operators with websites. There's even a funnel horn sound to welcome you.

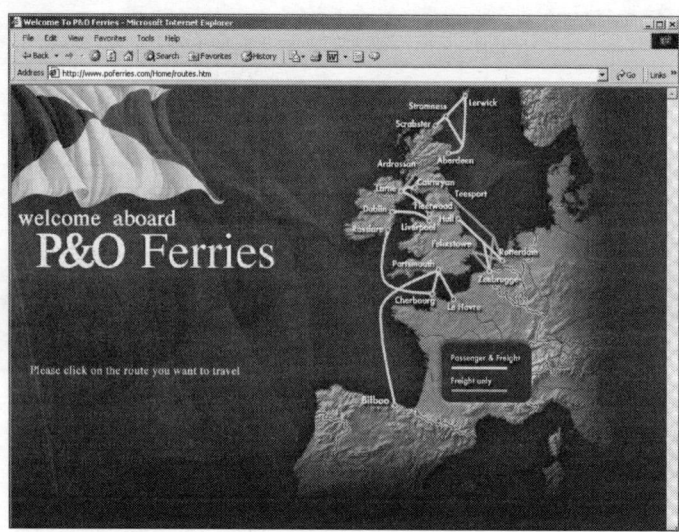

An easy-to-follow map on P&O Ferries' website (www.poferries.com) takes you directly to the ferry route you wish to travel with one click of the mouse; you can then book your tickets online.

Seafrance Online (www.seafrance.com)

These ferries go from Dover to Calais and back again. That's it. Got it? The only concession to fanciness is an online booking facility.

Ferry Savers (www.ferrysavers.com)

If you're looking for the cheapest possible crossing and you don't particularly care how or who you do it with, Ferry Savers will find it for you. You'll probably have to travel at unsociable hours, but if you're on a budget it's worth it.

Eurodrive (www.eurodrive.co.uk)

Eurodrive finds you the cheapest way to get your car to the Continent, whether that's by ferry or Channel Tunnel. It has a useful dynamic form that enables you to lower the quoted fares by altering the chosen times of departure.

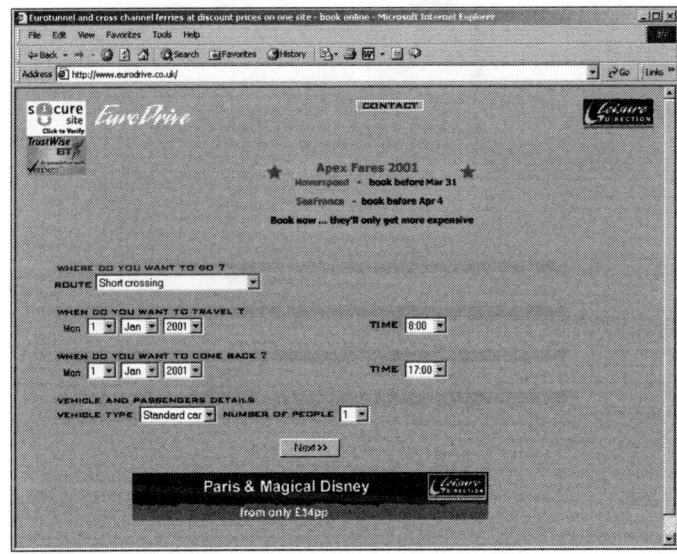

By whichever means you wish to take your car to the Continent, Eurodrive's website (www.eurodrive.co.uk) will find you the best deal.

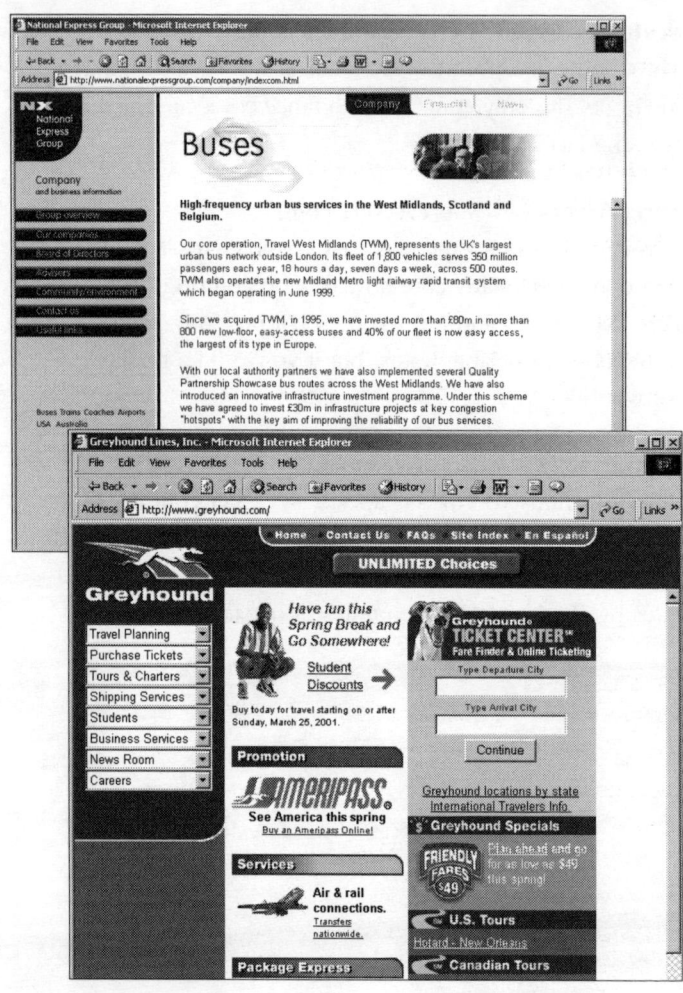

Coaches here and abroad: the National Express website (www.national expressgroup.com) includes timetables and up-to-the-minute discounts, while the vast network of Greyhound buses across the US, Canada and Mexico are detailed in their website (www.greyhound.com), together with suggested routes and specialist tours.

Bus and coach

Transport for London (www.londontransport.co.uk)
See page 12.

National Express (www.nationalexpressgroup.com)
The rapidly expanding National Express group now has
interests in buses, coaches, airports and trains at home
and internationally. Once at the corporate headquarters
site just click on the logo of the relevant company and
off you go. Online booking and special offers are there
for the taking.

Go-Ahead (www.go-ahead.com)
Go-Ahead is a glorified bus company with expansionist
ambitions, just like **First Group** (www.firstgroup.com) in
fact. Check out the routes and timetables and book online.

Busweb (www.busweb.co.uk)
If you're utterly dedicated to public transport, whether for
environmental or masochistic reasons, this site should satisfy
your cravings. There are links to scores of bus and coach
operators, plus related bus information sites both at home
and abroad.

Greyhound (www.greyhound.com)
The Greyhound bus must have appeared in more Hollywood
movies than John Wayne. If you hanker after a long bus
ride through the unfolding American landscape, Greyhound
buses are the only choice. The company operates more
than 20,000 daily departures to more than 3,700 locations
in the 48 contiguous United States, plus services to Canada
and Mexico.

Travel guides

Newsgroups

One thing the web does very well is provide a forum for sharing individual experiences. These days you don't have to rely on the opinions of one or two jaded guidebook writers, you can browse through the views of real people in chat rooms, newsgroups and website bulletin boards. It's much more interactive and dynamic and you can gain a vivid insight into the places you plan to visit.

These newsgroups are categorised according to subject and you can easily browse through the subject headings using the newsreader program incorporated in the latest versions of internet browsers. A good place to start looking is the Usenet search site **Google Groups** (http://groups. google.com), or simply open up your newsreader program and search the newsgroups listed on your internet service provider's server using relevant keywords. For example, there are several useful newsgroups in the **rec.travel** directory.

> **TIP**
>
> *An increasing number of online holiday sites and guides incorporate community bulletin boards on their sites, where visitors can post opinions and advice.*

An increasingly common feature is for online holiday sites and guides to incorporate community bulletin boards on their sites, where visitors can post opinions and advice. It's a useful way to encourage people to come back to the site.

Search engines and portal sites

The internet search engine and internet service provider portal sites also collate some useful links for the traveller. They usually aggregate information and services from other holiday sites and companies. For example, Excite's travel

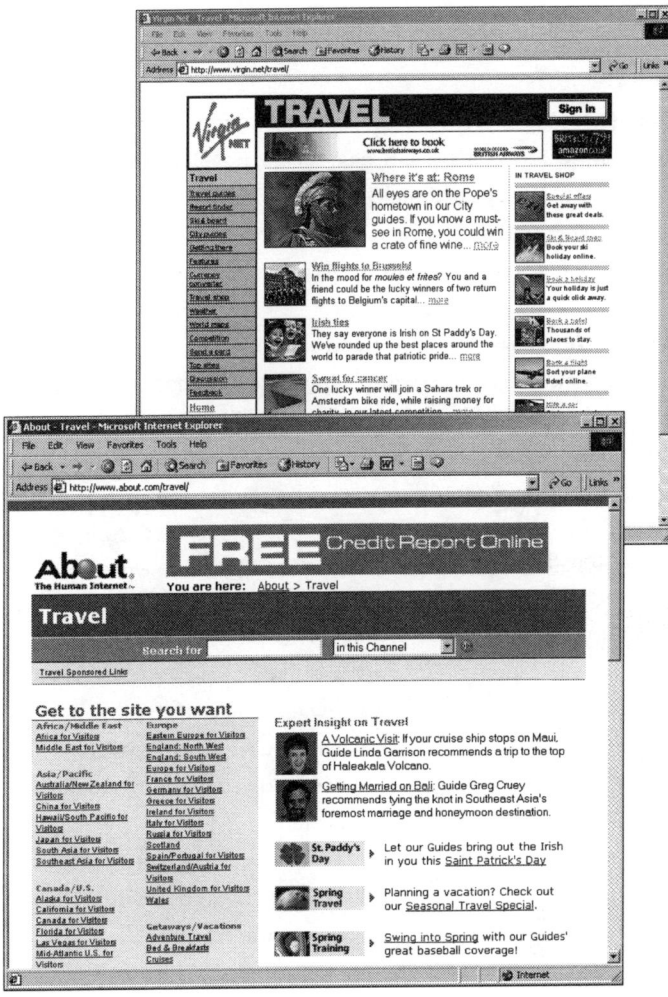

One of the best travel portals on the internet is Virgin Net (top, www.virgin.net/travel), covering everything from specialist holidays and hotel accommodation to maps and weather forecasts. The About.com search engine includes a travel section (bottom, www.about.com/travel) which provides quick and easy links to websites covering your area of choice.

section uses Thomas Cook for its flights information and
The First Resort for its package holiday bargains.

AOL (www.aol.co.uk)
AOL, the world's largest ISP, has its own travel 'channel' on its
proprietary service, with links to online holiday companies such
as Thomas Cook and Ebookers. It also has a range of its own
special offers with discounts available only to AOL members.

Virgin Net (www.virgin.net/travel)
This internet service provider's travel section contains a bagful
of travel-related services, including travel guides to countries
and cities, maps, a currency converter and weather
information from around the world.

Other travel sections worth checking out are:

About.com	www.about.com/travel
AltaVista	http://uk.altavista.com/content/travel/index.jsp
Excite	www.excite.co.uk/travel
Freeserve	www.freeserve.net/travel
Lycos	www.lycos.co.uk/webguides/travel
Search UK Travel	http://uk.searchengine.com
Yahoo!	http://uk.dir.yahoo.com/Recreation/Travel

General guides
Rough Guides (http://travel.roughguides.com)
The Rough Guides brand has become a world leader amongst
travellers. Its unique informative, yet informal, style has
endeared it to millions. The guides now cover over 14,000
destinations, searchable by country or city. An essential start
to anyone's holiday planning.

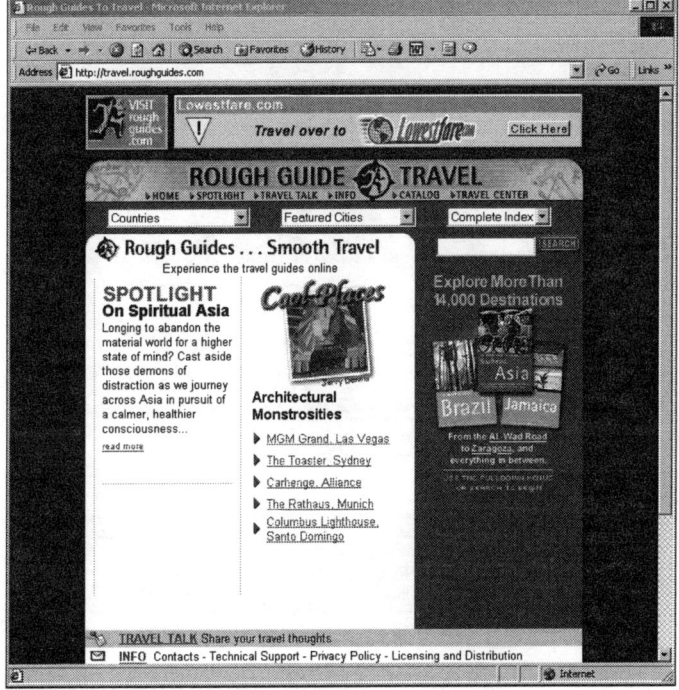

To check out the right guidebook for you or simply to read up on an area of interest, visit the Rough Guides website (http://travel.roughguides.com), which has successfully transferred their publishing expertise on to the internet.

Lonely Planet (www.lonelyplanet.com)

As well as its range of online travel guides, Lonely Planet also provides chat rooms for enthusiastic travellers where you can pick up invaluable tips and offer your own experiences and insights.

Concierge (www.concierge.com)

A US travel guide site featuring the Condé Nast *Traveler* magazine.

Experiencing the excitement of a spirited local event or avoiding the crowds during a festival season can make or break a holiday. These two websites (www.whatsonwhen.com and www.wwevents.com) cover the majority of annual happenings around the world.

Eurotrip (www.eurotrip.com)

This site is dedicated to European backpackers and contains a wealth of information, from hostel reviews to advice on how to bag yourself a cheap flight. The perfect site for a student taking a year off.

What's On When (www.whatsonwhen.com)

If you're looking for inspiration, a site organised around world events should give you some ideas for interesting holidays. It lists all the festivals, games, carnivals and exhibitions happening around the world to give your holiday an activity focus.

World Wide Events (www.wwevents.com)

In a similar vein, World Wide Events lets you browse through a comprehensive list of global shindigs. Just select a country and month and browse through the cultural, sporting and leisure events. There isn't too much information to go on, though the database is updated daily.

Worldwide Holiday & Festival Page (www.holiday festival.com)

If you've ever fancied running with the bulls in Spain, or watching the wild horse race in Siena, Italy, this site will help you make sure you don't get there too late.

Travel Guides for Tourists with Disabilities (http://europa.eu.int/comm/dg23/tourism/tourism-publications/travel_guides.html)

With such a snappy title, this site could only come from the European Commission. Don't expect jazzy design or humourous banter, but there is a set of downloadable

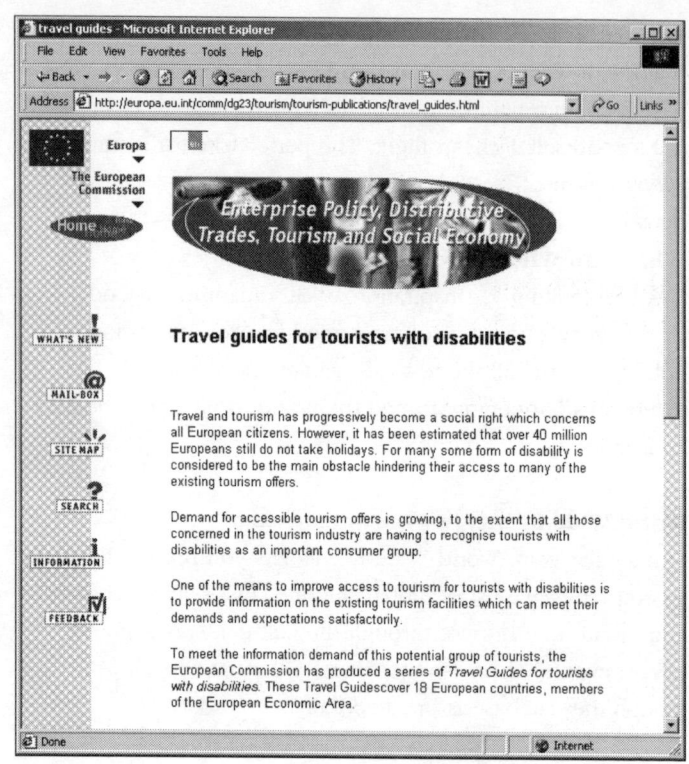

Europa
The European
Commission
Home

**Enterprise Policy, Distributive
Trades, Tourism and Social Economy**

WHAT'S NEW

MAIL-BOX

SITE MAP

SEARCH

INFORMATION

FEEDBACK

Travel guides for tourists with disabilities

Travel and tourism has progressively become a social right which concerns all European citizens. However, it has been estimated that over 40 million Europeans still do not take holidays. For many some form of disability is considered to be the main obstacle hindering their access to many of the existing tourism offers.

Demand for accessible tourism offers is growing, to the extent that all those concerned in the tourism industry are having to recognise tourists with disabilities as an important consumer group.

One of the means to improve access to tourism for tourists with disabilities is to provide information on the existing tourism facilities which can meet their demands and expectations satisfactorily.

To meet the information demand of this potential group of tourists, the European Commission has produced a series of *Travel Guides for tourists with disabilities*. These Travel Guidescover 18 European countries, members of the European Economic Area.

Done   Internet

*A long-winded but useful website (http://europa.eu.int/comm/dg23/
tourism/tourism-publications/travel_guides.html) for travellers with
disabilities visiting Europe, offering information on accommodation,
attractions and more with disabled facilities.*

booklets in PDF format (you need to download Adobe
Acrobat Reader to read this kind of file – **www.adobe.com**).
These booklets, covering 18 European countries, give
details of tourist destinations that cater to the needs of
disabled people. A lot of the information is equally relevant
to all travellers. There are lots of useful contacts, and despite
the dryness of tone, this is still a useful site to help you
plan your holiday.

Guides to Britain

Britannia Travels (http://britannia.com/travel)

This is an excellent all-round guide and holiday booking site for the UK traveller. It crams in all sorts of guides and other resources, such as a UK phone book, hotel finder and car rental section.

Visit Britain (www.visitbritain.com)

This is the official home of the British Tourist Authority, where you can explore the many delights our islands have to offer. The site comes up with plenty of its own holiday ideas, from cycling to themed holidays, such as visiting places featured in famous films. There are interactive maps, tips and guides galore on this well-organised site.

About Britain (www.aboutbritain.com)

This guide site organises its information around events and attractions, giving you ideas about what to see and do. From historic houses to amusement parks, art exhibitions to famous gardens, About Britain will give you no end of inspiration.

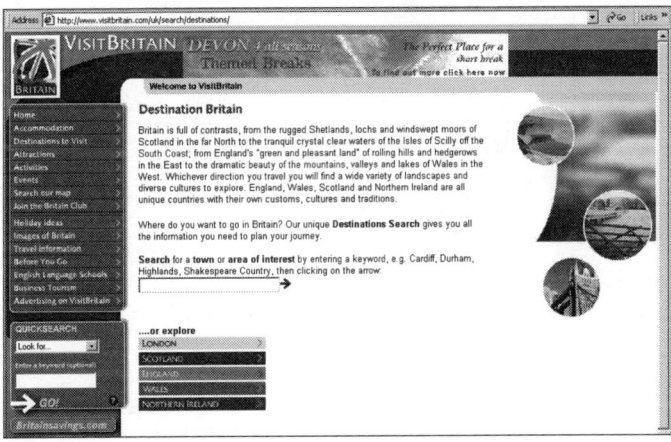

There is little a visitor to Britain can wish to learn about the country that isn't detailed on the Tourist Authority website (www.visitbritain.com).

Brochures

Holiday Wizard (www.holidaywizard.co.uk)

If you still like the idea of flicking through holiday brochures
with all those pictures of beautiful smiling people in sunny
places, the web can help. You don't have to go to your local
travel agent and load up with glossies. Holiday Wizard lets
you peruse many brochures online, join the e-mail mailing list
so you're kept up-to-date with developments, and make an
e-mail request for hard copy brochures. The main advantage
is that the site lists brochures from the specialist holiday
companies as well as the major brand names, giving you
more choice in one convenient location. You can browse
by holiday type or destination.

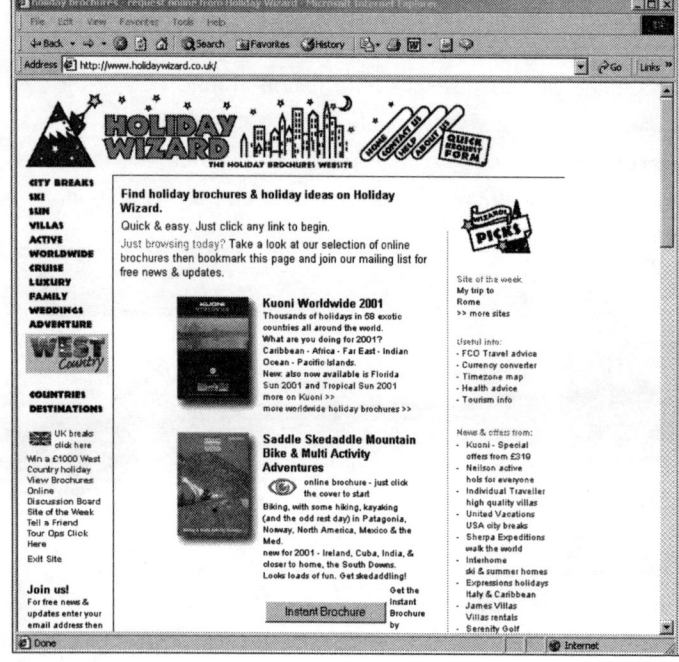

*A visit to a high street travel agent from the comfort of your own home –
this useful site (www.holidaywizard.co.uk) not only screens pages from
holiday brochures but allows you to order copies via e-mail.*

Route planners

Automobile Association (www.theaa.com)

As well as all the usual information about the breakdown and recovery services the AA offers members, the site has an excellent Travelwatch section, comprising a route planner and up-to-the-minute news on the country's congested road network. The route planner includes estimated mileages and journey times, adjusted according to whether you're towing a caravan, for example.

RAC (www.rac.co.uk)

You can find out the latest traffic news region by region across the country from the RAC. Again, refreshing your browser from time to time ensures that the information you're seeing is bang up-to-date. There is also a useful route planner to help you select the fastest or shortest route to take.

Green Flag (www.greenflag.co.uk)

Breakdown company Green Flag also offers route planners for the UK and Europe, plus driving guides and advice on driving abroad. As with the AA, Green Flag incorporates a travel insurance quotation service, plus a ferry and Channel Tunnel booking service.

Michelin (www.michelin-travel.com)

French tyre-manufacturer Michelin has also made a name for itself as a travel and gourmet guide specialist. Its travel site is a useful stop-off if you're planning a trans-European odyssey. You can plot your route, find good hotels and restaurants, and learn about toll roads.

PetrolBusters.com (www.petrolbusters.com)

If you're concerned about finding the cheapest place to buy your petrol, PetrolBusters (produced in conjunction with the

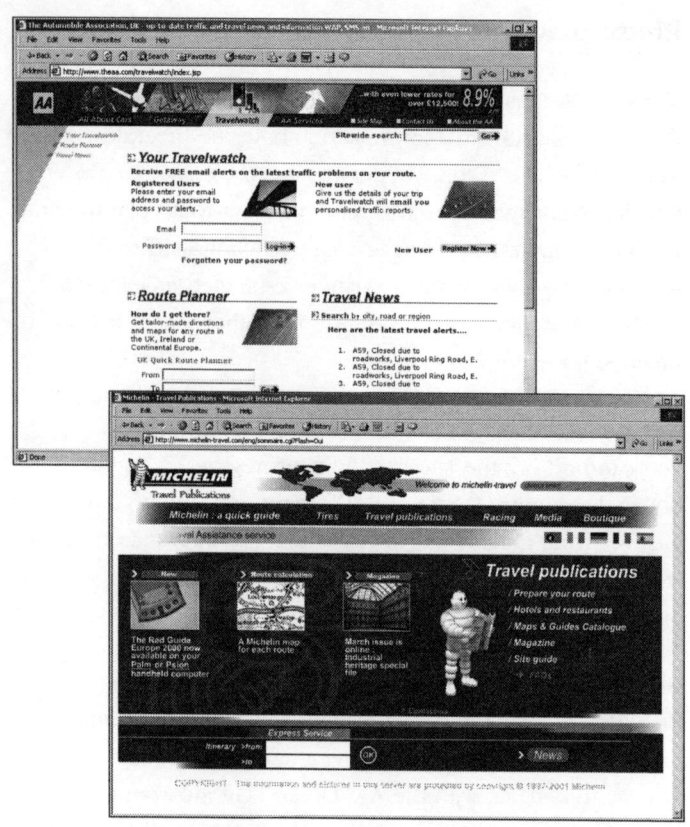

If you're planning a road journey in the UK, check out the AA's website (top, www.theaa.com) before departure. Details of traffic hold-ups and alternative routes are updated at regular intervals. If you're travelling in Europe, the renowned Michelin group's website (bottom, www.michelin-travel.com) includes journey planning, local attractions and sports.

AA) does the shopping around for you. Just register, type in your postcode, and up pop the lowest prices offered by the garages in your area. Over a year the difference between the cheapest and the most expensive can add up to hundreds of pounds.

Maps

Part of the fun of travel is working out the route you're going to take and the terrain you're going to pass over or through. Unfolding the map and spreading it on the kitchen table is one method. Accessing an online world map site is another. These days you can access detailed maps of almost any country in the world, usually for free. Before too long we'll be accessing these resources using integrated personal organisers and mobile phones. They'll probably also have global positioning system (GPS) gizmos built in enabling us to pinpoint exactly where we are on the planet via satellite.

In the meantime, here are some useful map sites:

Mapquest	www.mapquest.com
Virgin Net	www.virgin.net/travel/ world_maps
Multimedia Mapping	www.multimap.com
Map Machine	www.nationalgeographic.com/ resources/ngo/maps
Maps.com	www.maps.com

Weather

Before setting off on a long car journey it can also be a good idea to check the weather forecast just in case you're heading into a blizzard or other potentially hazardous driving conditions. If you're longing to escape the gloomy UK weather, it's pretty important to check out the temperature of your chosen destination. And, of course, the most weather-conscious holidaymakers are the skiers. For some, ignorance of the weather conditions could jeopardise their lives.

For the most authoritative UK forecasts go to the **Meteorological Office** (www.met-office.gov.uk). It offers a

Simply type in a street name, city name and country almost anywhere in the world and Mapquest will instantly produce a detailed map of the area on your computer screen as well as directing you to the location.

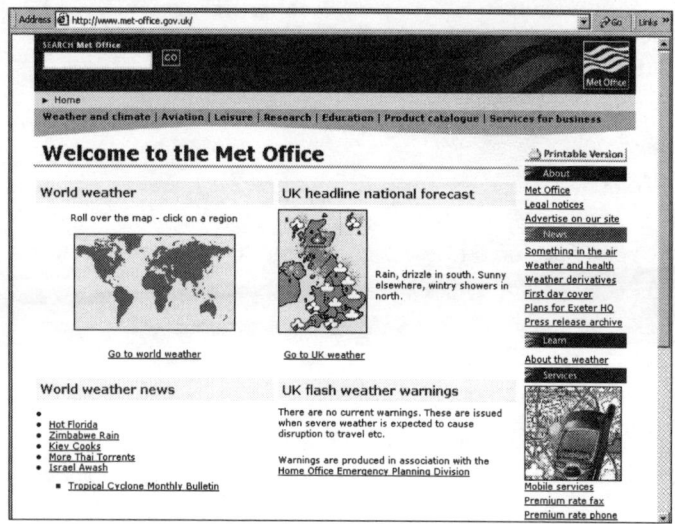

London's Met Office has a well-organised website (www.met-office.gov.uk) covering forecasts not only for weather in the UK and abroad, but current conditions for recreational pursuits such as flying and hiking.

well-designed site with three-day forecasts for each region. When the weather is bad there are specific weather warnings, too. The Met Office also provides forecasts for foreign countries, to help you plan your holiday route.

Another useful website, specialising in US weather, is **AccuWeather** (www.accuweather.com). You can see sophisticated satellite weather maps of the whole of the USA in real-time.

A lot of general travel and holiday sites have weather sections these days, so keeping abreast of conditions abroad has never been easier.

Complaints

Before you go ahead and book a holiday you may want to check out the reputation of the company you're booking with. **Holiday Complaints** (www.holiday complaints.com) is a database of complaints from holidaymakers against various travel operators. If your chosen company appears on the list you may want to think twice about booking. But use your discretion, as there's no way of verifying whether the complaints are well founded or not. The usefulness of such a site will very much depend on the number of people who contribute to it.

Learning the lingo

Learning a few phrases of the local lingo is always a good idea before you travel abroad, if only to get you out of a tight spot in an emergency. Of course, the pocket dictionary will come in handy for such essential phrases as 'my postilion has been struck by lightning', but the web can be handy for self-help lessons before setting off. It won't be long before

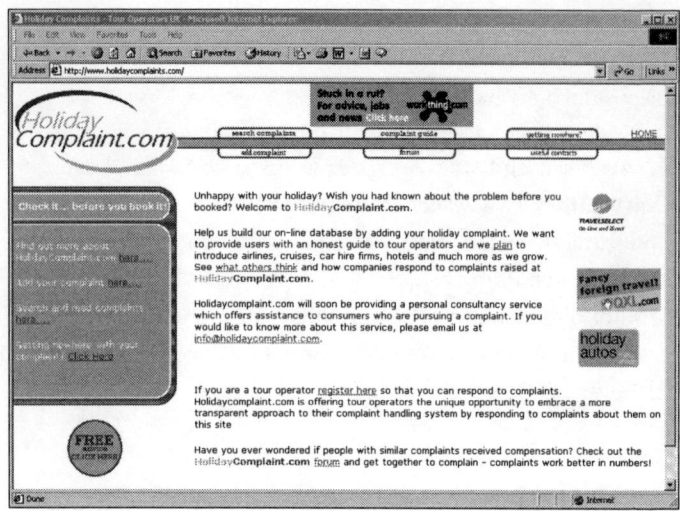

A forum-style website (www.holidaycomplaints.com) where travellers can exchange holiday horror stories and check the reputation of travel companies based on clients' experiences.

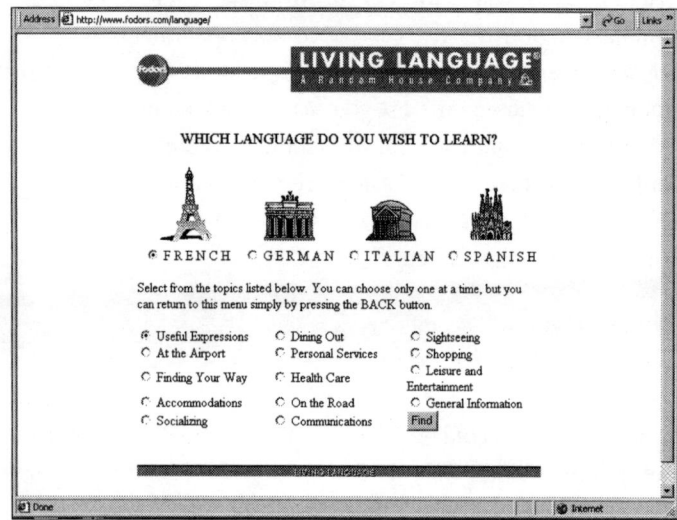

Online phrase books such as this one produced by Fodors (www.fodors. com/language) offer all the usual words and phrases required by tourists, in four languages.

we're all trotting round the globe carrying our integrated hand-held computers-cum-mobile-phones, accessing electronic dictionaries on the hoof.

Fodor's Living Language (www.fodors.com/language)
Collates useful expressions to learn in French, German, Italian and Spanish. The expressions are categorised according to common holiday activities, such as dining and shopping. Pronunciations are spelt out phonetically.

Travlang (www.travlang.com)
Contains a whole host of online language dictionaries (including Esperanto) with easy look-up facilities.

Health and safety information

Now that modern technology has given us the opportunity to travel to far-flung places around the globe, we also have the chance to contract some really interesting diseases into the bargain. Knowing what jabs to have and what health precautions to take is obviously important. Luckily, there are a few excellent advice sites around to keep us healthy while on holiday.

Fit For Travel (www.fitfortravel.scot.nhs.uk/Home.html)
Compiled and updated by a team of experts from the Travel Medicine Division at the Scottish Centre for Infection and Environmental Health, the site includes maps showing regions where malaria is common, for example, as well as a country-by-country breakdown of health information.

Department of Health (www.doh.gov.uk/traveladvice)
As you would expect, there is lots of useful advice here on required immunisations, recommended diet, and how to fill in

the Form E111 to ensure free access to healthcare in an emergency in countries that are part of the European Union. You don't always need an E111, so check this site first. You can pick up the form from any local post office.

The Foreign Office (www.fco.gov.uk)

For general advice on places to avoid altogether – unless you have a yen for kidnapping and civil war as part of your rest and relaxation plans – the newly revamped Foreign & Commonwealth Office site is definitely worth a look. As well as the usual country-specific advice, there's information about British Consular services abroad and how you can get hold of an English-speaking lawyer should you find yourself in a Turkish clink after a particularly energetic night out. Flippancy aside, this site could save your life.

This informative site (www.fitfortravel.scot.nhs.uk/Home.html) details any inoculations or other health precautions required by travellers going abroad, both prior to leaving home and during their trip.

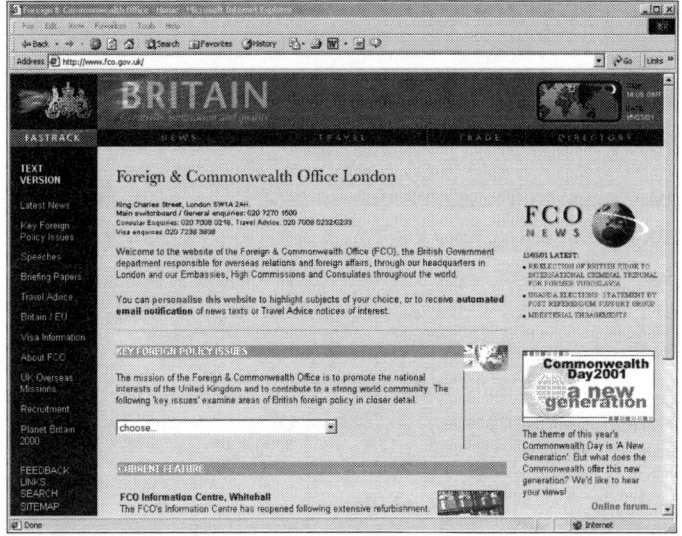

The British Foreign Office now offers its advice to UK travellers online (www.fco.gov.uk), from the serious issue of no-go areas to the practical details of finding English-speaking representation abroad.

Passports

UK Passport Agency (www.ukpa.gov.uk)

The last thing you want to do after all the usual holiday planning is turn up at the airport with an out-of-date passport. The UK Passport Agency's site gives comprehensive information on how to apply for, renew or amend a UK passport. Application packs can be ordered and there are listings for regional UKPA offices. Current turnaround times are shown and the Passport Application Tracker provides an e-mail contact to check the progress of urgent applications.

Travelling with pets

Pet Travel Scheme (www.maff.gov.uk/animalh/quarantine)
The Ministry of Agriculture Fisheries and Food website tells
you everything you need to know about getting your pet
microchipped for identification purposes when travelling
abroad under the new Pet Travel Scheme. You also have to
see that your pet is vaccinated and has a blood test before
setting off. Plus, there's advice on how to look after your pet
in transit.

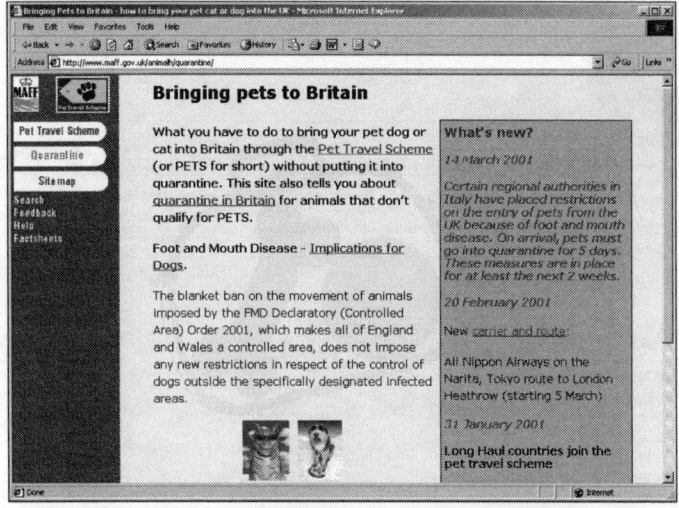

*With Britain's quarantine laws slowly becoming more relaxed, this is the
official site offering up-to-date information on taking pets in and out of the
UK (www.maff.gov.uk/animalh/quarantine).*

Chapter 3

Flights

Researching and booking flights is the most popular travel-related activity on the web. Airlines, especially the discount operations, are finding that the web is a powerful tool for selling seats at low cost. Discounters Ryanair and easyJet sold roughly half their tickets online in the year 2000, and the proportion of total airline tickets being sold this way is growing fast.

FACT

The travel market in Europe alone is estimated to grow to around £8 billion by the end of 2002 and flights will account for roughly a third of that.

The world of airline seats is a complicated one. You'd think that a seat on a plane came at a set price. Not so. It's quite common for two people to be sitting next to each other on the same flight having paid radically different amounts. We don't need to go into all the ins and outs of the business here, but suffice it to say that in such a fluid market dictated by the laws of supply and demand, it pays to shop around and be flexible in your travel arrangements.

With so many airlines competing for so many routes and schedules, the web has become the perfect tool for interrogating massive 'real-time' databases, for the industry and the travelling public. The most common flight specialists on the web are so-called consolidators – companies that buy blocks of seats from the airlines then try to sell them on to us. But almost all travel websites contain a flights section these days.

In this chapter we give you lots of flight-related web resources, including airports and airlines, online travel agents and flight auction sites, with tips on how to find the cheapest fares around.

Airports

BAA (www.baa.co.uk)

British Airports Authority proudly claims to be the world's leading airport company. As it owns Heathrow, Gatwick, Stansted, Glasgow, Edinburgh, Aberdeen and Southampton airports, you can see why. The corporate HQ site has links to all these airports, with flight timetables, online shopping and other services, such as pre-booking of airport car-parking spaces and foreign currency ordering. You can organise upgrades, too, and book holidays, hotels and car rental through links with partner sites, such as Expedia, Lastminute.com and Hotelink.

A2bAirports (www.a2bairports.com)

A2bAirports features all the airports in the UK and Ireland, with terminal guides, maps telling you how to get there, plus driving directions, and contact telephone numbers for local taxi, bus and train services. You also get up-to-the-minute flight arrival information and the very latest holiday departure price and availability details. There are 43 airports listed. You can book tickets online through its sister site, **A2Btravel.com** (*see page 45*).

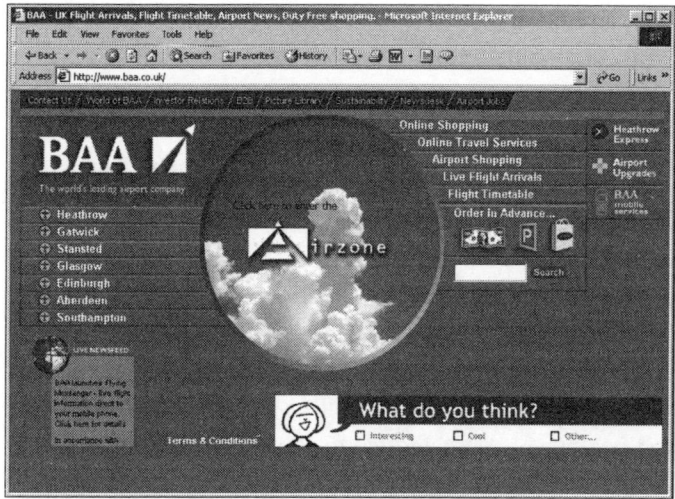

The busy network of airports around Britain is brought together on one website by the British Airport Authority (www.baa.co.uk), offering a variety of pre-bookable services within the airports.

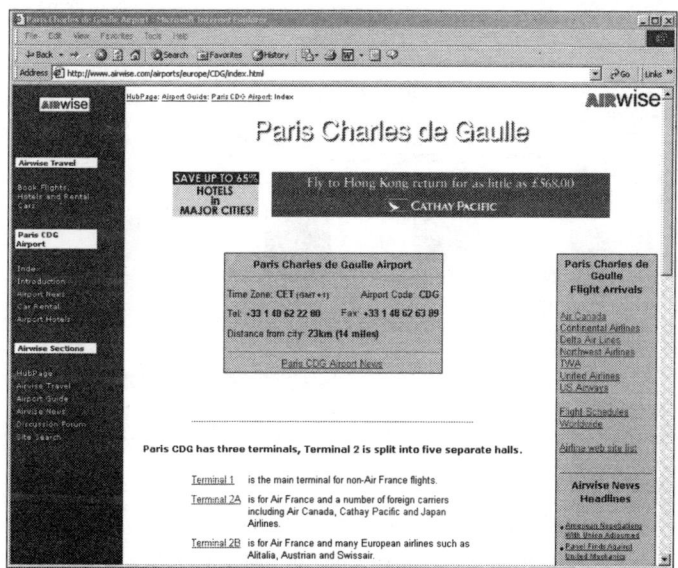

A guide to airports around the world (www.airwise.com/airports/index.html), including very useful floor plans of terminals.

Airwise Airport Guide

(http://www.airwise.com/airports/index.html)

This international guide provides general advice on the world's airports and their facilities. You search by region. There's also a list of the world's top 50 airports with links through to them all.

Airlines

If the airline you fly with is more important than finding the cheapest fare, you may as well go straight to its website and book there. More and more airlines are incorporating online booking into their sites and some offer discounts for booking online, too.

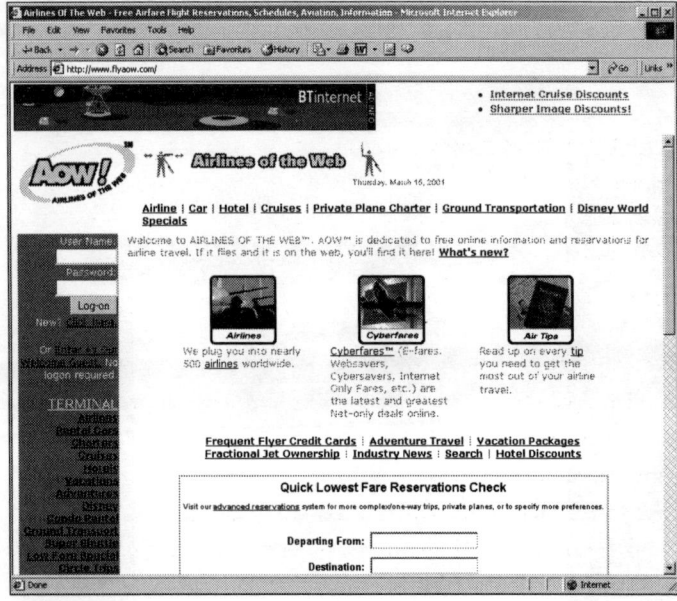

Details of every major airline in the world, as well as numerous smaller charter firms, are brought together in one comprehensive website (www.flyaow.com).

Airlines of the Web (www.flyaow.com)
For a comprehensive guide to the world's airlines, go to this
site and stay there. This is an excellent tool for detailed
planning of your worldwide odyssey. Not all the airlines offer
online booking, though. There are also plenty of links to
other travel-related websites.

A2Btravel.com (www.a2btravel.com/airlines.html)
This excellently resourced site gives links to all the
world's airlines in A–Z format. It uses Travelocity and
Bargainholidays.com as its flight-booking services.

British Airways (www.british-airways.com)
The UK's premier airline contains everything you need to
plan and book your flight, including a list of its special offers
and booking tips. Take these with a big pinch of salt though,
as an airline might have a vested interest in encouraging you
to 'book well in advance'. So much for last-minute bargains!

British Midland (www.flybmi.com)
British Midland's well-designed site includes online booking
and web-only special offers. It was the first UK airline to
experiment with auctioning its tickets in one-off time-limited
events. Definitely a company to watch.

Virgin Atlantic (www.fly-virgin.com)
Virgin's Flash-heavy website takes a while to load and is
organised along world regional lines. The design actually
hampers rather than helps in that the writing is actually quite
hard to read. Nevertheless, if you persevere you can do all
the usual things and there are some holiday ideas as well.

United Airlines (www.ual.com)
This is a very well-stocked website, as you might expect from
one of the world's biggest airlines. As well as timetables and

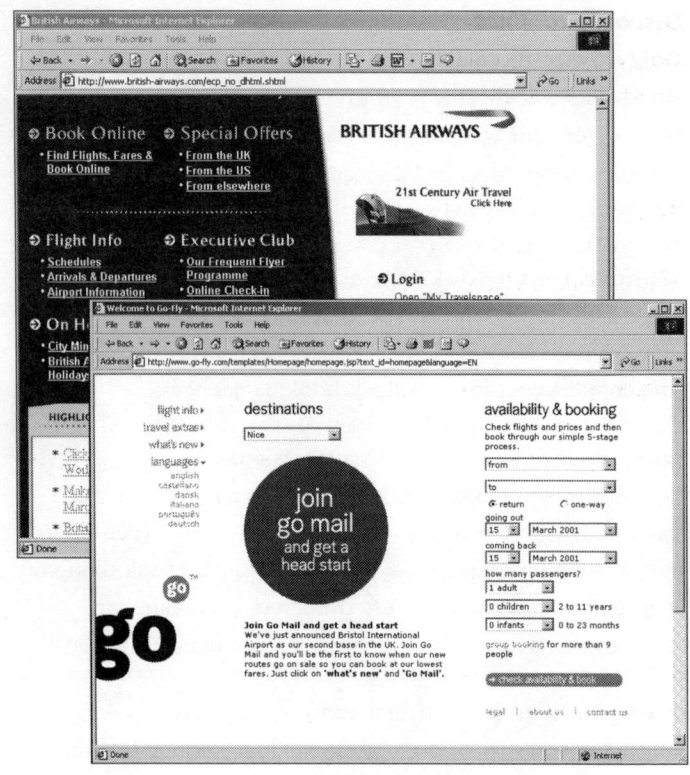

As you might expect from one of the world's largest airlines, the British Airways website (top, www.british-airways.com) provides all the necessary information on flights, bookings and special offers. For cheap flights, check out the website of British Airways' discount airline Go! (bottom, www.go-fly.com). Hip design and easy navigation, not to mention the low prices, make this website a pleasure to use.

online booking facilities, there are travel guides and frequent-flyer reward schemes, plus car rental and hotel services. Its last-minute online bargains are called E-Fares, but you have to register first to access details.

Discount airlines

Go! (www.go-fly.com)

British Airways' discount operation was launched as a result of fierce competition from cut-price rivals such as easyJet. Since then they've been finding it tough going in this low-margin market. The site is beautifully simple yet functional, and there's a £2 discount if you book online. I just wish they'd make it clearer how you secure the quoted special offer fares.

Virgin Express (www.virgin-express.com)

Competition forced Virgin to reduce the routes offered by its discount service, concentrating on Brussels as the main hub, travelling to major European destinations from there. The only route from London is to Brussels, thereafter you have to change planes. A cut-down service and a cut-down website.

easyJet (www.easyjet.com)

The bane of the established airlines and known for its ebullient and publicity-seeking boss, Stelios Haji-Ioannou, easyJet has done a lot to rejuvenate the UK's regional airports. This is how it keeps its prices low. Booking a return trip online wins you a £5 discount.

Ryanair (www.ryanair.com)

Although the prices displayed on Ryanair's site seem ridiculously low, it is not immediately clear how you buy flights at those prices. If you click on one of the advertised fares you're taken through to a booking section. Key in the dates you want to travel and invariably the actual price comes out much higher. Nevertheless, you can get some amazing deals if you dig deep enough.

Buzz (www.buzzaway.com)

Another low-cost airline focusing on routes from London Stansted to various European short-haul destinations. Prices quoted are one-way and are not refundable. You can book online and decide whether you want a meal with your flight (for which you pay extra).

Flight sites

This is where it gets complicated. For a start, there are myriad travel sites out there offering flights. The choice is bewildering. Some simply publish all the quoted airline fares, others specialise in rooting out last-minute bargains. The flight prices themselves are often wrapped up in ribbons of conditions. For example, you may find that special offer tickets have to be bought at least five days in advance or are not available at weekends.

There's no single easy way to find cheap fares, because there are so many variables involved in reaching the final price you see on screen. What's more, the price you see isn't necessarily the price you'll get. It all depends on what day and what time you want to travel.

WARNING

Bear in mind that in many cases quoted fares won't include airport taxes. These can take the shine off an apparent bargain pretty quickly.

But the great thing about using an online flight agent is that it does most of the shopping around for you. If you go direct to an airline you can never be sure you're getting the best price.

Then again, not all the online agents will have access to all the available prices. So it pays to try several online agents and go direct as well, just to make sure.

If you follow our checklist at the end of this section (*see page 62*) you'll have a good chance of landing yourself some decent bargains.

Expedia (www.expedia.co.uk)

Software company Microsoft's online travel agent is one of the best-known on the web. Just select where you want to fly from and to, the dates and times, the number of people travelling, and away you go. Expedia lists all the cheapest prices published by the airlines and the attendant terms and conditions. These aren't necessarily the cheapest anywhere, though, and seats may not be available on the days you want to travel. The site also features a 'Fare Compare' section that lets you see what prices other Expedia users have managed to achieve for the same flights. Plus, there's a bargain fares section with a selection of the best prices to popular destinations.

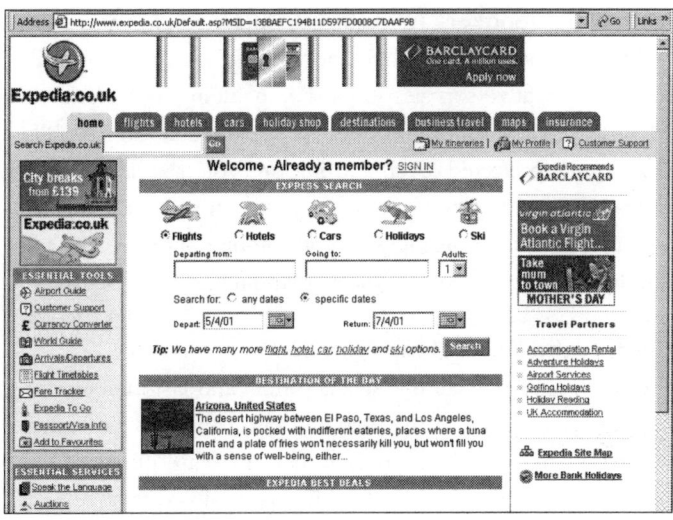

This online travel agent (www.expedia.co.uk) offers all the services you would expect from a high street agency, from flights, to car rental, to package deals.

Travelocity (www.travelocity.co.uk)

Travelocity, owned by travel database group Sabre, lets you search for flights in a number of ways. You can be as specific or as flexible as you like. Obviously the more flexible you are the more chance there is of you bagging a cheap flight. Once you've chosen a flight, a calendar page shows you the dates you can travel at that price. Click on your chosen dates and the systems also tells you if there are still seats left on that plane. If not, it shows you the next available dates. You can buy the tickets online there and then. Frequent visitors to the site have to register and become members. It's all very impressive.

Ebookers (www.ebookers.com)

Ebookers is in the premier league of online travel agents and the most popular European agent on the web, according to analyst research in January 2001. Its flight ticketing service is run by **Flightbookers (www.flightbookers.co.uk)**. There's a 24-hour customer service helpline. Ebookers has introduced several innovative services to its site, including 'fare alert', which lets you know if the price for a particular journey falls below your preferred level, and informs you if an airline is prepared to offer you a seat at your chosen price. Ebookers will also send text messages to your mobile phone giving you the flight status of a plane you're planning to meet or catch.

Cheapflights (www.cheapflights.com)

This site aggregates all the special offers and last-minute bargains it can find on the web and elsewhere. If cost, rather than convenience, is the priority, then there are plenty of bargains to be found with Cheapflights. It also offers bargains on holidays, accommodation and insurance.

There are a number of websites specialising in discount airfares, including the flights section of Ebookers (top, www.flightbookers.co.uk), www.bargainholidays.com (center) and www.dhf.co.uk (bottom).

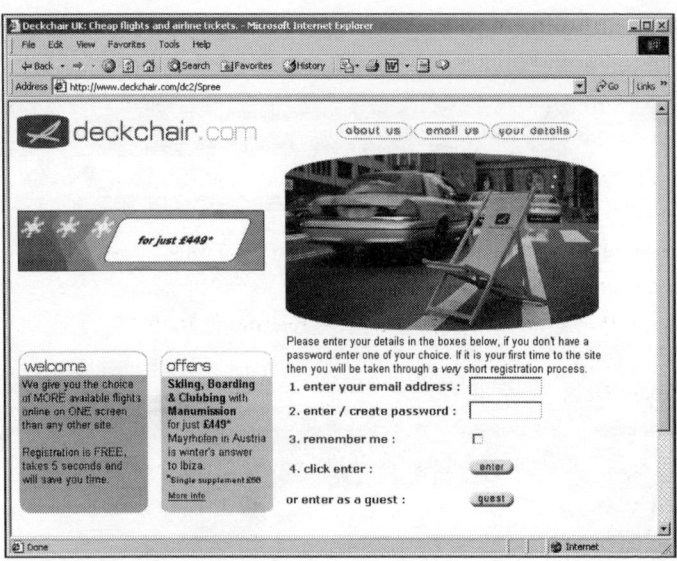

Sir Bob Geldof showed his characteristic verve in setting up a simple and efficient flight directory (www.deckchair.com) when he was dissatisfied with other sites he found on the net.

Dial-A-Flight (www.dialaflight.com)

Dial-A-Flight claims to offer four million flight bargains on its site, as well as holiday offers. It is the UK's second-largest flight retailer and has been in business for over 20 years. Its site receives some half a million visitors a month. Just type where you want to go and when, and it comes up with the cheapest flight it can find. If you like what you see, you ring up and book. Simple. If you give your e-mail address you can receive newsletters giving details of the latest offers.

Lastminute.com (www.lastminute.com)

Despite marketing itself as an 'impulse buy' site, Lastminute does also carry advance details of flights, as well as its last-minute special offers. Its search engine and online application form is dynamic and intuitive, making the search process a relative doddle.

Bargainholidays (www.bargainholidays.com)

This all-round holiday and travel site also has a dedicated flights-only section, with separate search facilities for chartered and scheduled flights. The flights data is actually supplied by **A2Bflights** (www.a2bflights.com). At the time of writing (February 2001) scheduled flights could not be booked online due to an incompatibility problem with the Internet Explorer 5.5 web browser and booking had to be made through the Bargainholidays telephone team.

Deckchair (www.deckchair.com)

Sir Bob Geldof reportedly founded this site after getting fed up with what else was on offer. It may not be particularly fancy, but it does list deals from over 500 airlines flying to 9,000 airports around the world.

Just The Ticket (www.justtheticket.co.uk)

Describing themselves as 'the discount flight specialists', **Just The Ticket** claim to offer over one million discount flights and holidays. You can search scheduled and charter flight databases and book online. It's not sophisticated, but it does the job.

Air Tickets Direct (www.booking.airtickets.co.uk)

I like this site. It may look as if it was designed by a five-year-old, but that just gives it a refreshing simplicity. The prices quoted seemed quite competitive to me and it presented the information in a way that was easy to understand. It gave a price for the whole travelling party and included all relevant taxes and insurance. Bookings less than ten days in advance have to be completed by phone.

Sky Deals (www.skydeals.co.uk)

Sky Deals provides the flights service for **The First Resort** (www.firstresort.com), part of the Thomson travel group.

It brings together special offers and published prices on chartered and scheduled flights. Booking online wins you a £5 discount. You can register and receive e-mail newsletters detailing the latest special deals. The site is admirably simple and well designed, although I suspect that if you're not flexible on the dates you can travel, you're unlikely to find a bargain here.

Airline Network (www.airnet.co.uk)

A well-organised site backed by an established travel company staffed by some 150 consultants. As such, the site also gives details of short breaks and other holidays.

Discount Holidays and Flights (www.dhf.co.uk)

When you key the dates you want to travel, this site asks you if you're prepared to be flexible and travel on other days if it is cheaper to do so. This is a very useful innovation. A lot of other website databases aren't so flexible. The search data is supplied by TelMe Global Traveller and ticket sales are handled by Seaforths Travel Ltd.

Cheap and cheerful
International Association of Air Travel Couriers (UK) (www.aircourier.co.uk)

If you don't mind doing a little bit of work in return for massive savings on scheduled courier flights, then joining the IAATC is worthwhile. The courier usually carries a small package of documents but also has the normal baggage allowance. Discounts of up to 75% are possible. The IAATC, based in Florida, USA, but with a European office in the UK, has over 10,000 members worldwide. IAATC keeps track of every courier company in the world that requires couriers and regularly distributes this information to its members.

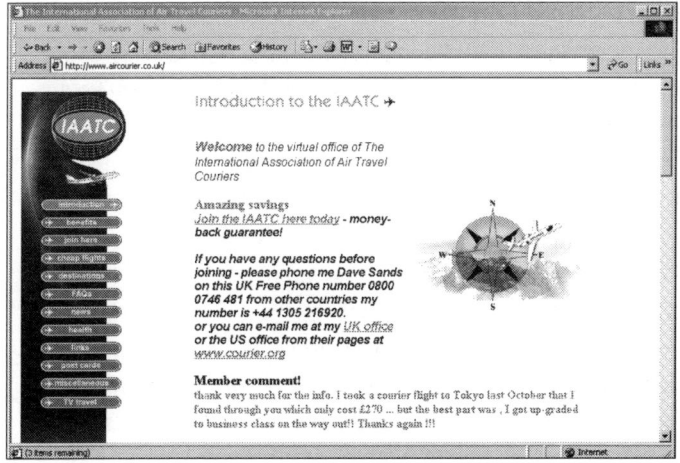

Working as a courier of important documents between various international destinations can offer incredible savings on flights, but you have to pay to join this official website (www. aircourier.co.uk) before you can qualify.

Information on last-minute flights is also posted daily on its website. The annual membership charge is £32 and you can pay online. If you plan to do a lot of travelling and you're serious about saving money, this is a very good idea.

Flight auctions

Conventional auctions

Online auctions have taken off in a big way across all categories of product. The web has made it relatively easy for people to carry out person-to-person auctions and for companies to flog excess inventory to the highest bidder.

Once you register with an online auction site you browse the categories looking through all the available lots. If something takes your fancy, you can place a bid there and then by giving your credit card details. Bids tend to go up in set increments, and you can often tell the system to increase your bids automatically up to your ceiling price. This means you don't have to stay glued to your screen all day, watching to see if you've been outbid. This is just as well seeing as auctions can last days and even weeks. Each lot will have accompanying information telling you how much time is left before the auction is closed. The later you leave it, the less chance there is of being outbid.

Before you commit yourself to the bidding process, check out the conditions. You may find that you can't travel at a convenient time, or you may have to stay a certain number of nights.

UK airline operator **British Midland** (www.flybmi.com) has already hosted several ticket auctions, with travellers bidding in the hope of bagging a bargain. Other airlines are flirting with the idea. But the main auction website to go to is:

QXL Ricardo (www.qxl.com/uk)
Go to the Travel Shop section of the site, click on 'Flights', and see what's on offer. Of course, it's easy to get carried away in an auction and end up bidding more than you would pay through an online discounter. So make sure you have an idea of the typical cost of the flight you're after. If you don't particularly care where you go, you're more likely to strike it lucky. When I checked, I found tickets to New York costing £160 with only two hours to go before the auction closed. Very tempting.

WARNING

Before you commit yourself to the bidding process in an auction, check out the conditions. You may find that you can't travel at a convenient time, or you may have to stay a certain number of nights.

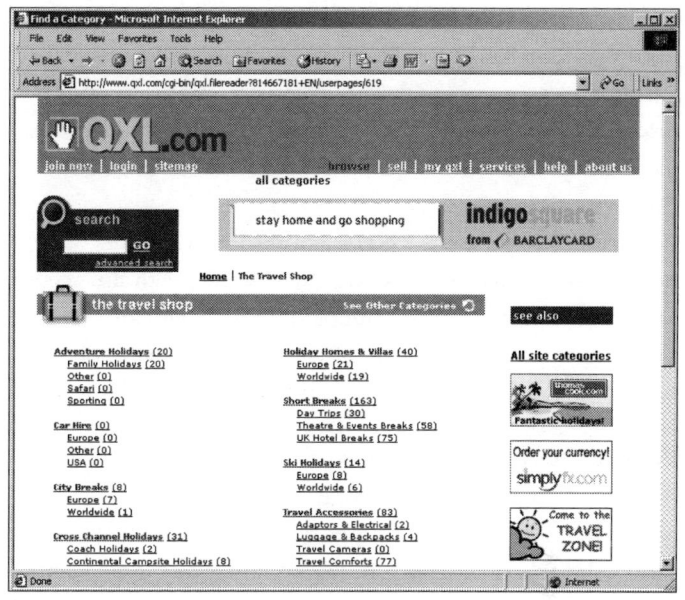

This auction website (www.qxl.com/uk) has a travel section with flight prices open to bidding, as well as other travel related lots.

Reverse auctions

The reverse auction is a new twist on the auction concept. Instead of bidders competing against each other, you indicate a price you are prepared to pay and then wait to see if any provider is willing to take you up on your offer. It originated in the USA, of course, but is beginning to gain a foothold in the UK, largely thanks to its main proponent, Priceline (*see next page*).

(*see next page*)

FACT

Industry estimates are that there are around 100,000 empty seats on planes leaving the UK every day.

The reverse auction works on the basis that airlines have trouble filling their planes in all the slots they have available, as most people are generally unwilling to travel at inconvenient times. An airline may also want to draw attention to a new route that it operates by releasing some tickets cheaply as a promotion. Industry estimates suggest that there are around 100,000 empty seats on planes leaving the UK every day.

These seats are up for grabs at a price that can be negotiated between the passenger and airline, with the agent acting as intermediary. For intrepid travellers who are prepared to put up with a bit of discomfort in return for a bargain fare, such services are a godsend.

Priceline (www.priceline.co.uk)

Priceline pioneered the concept of consumers setting the price for airline tickets and other goods and services. Priceline Europe launched its service in the UK in January 2001 with a major TV advertising campaign, claiming that you can save up to 40% on the best prices available elsewhere.

All you do is decide how much you are prepared to pay for a particular flight, enter it on the website or ring Priceline's freephone number (0800 074 5000), and it then interrogates the airlines to see if there are any takers.

Of course, the difficulty with this kind of reverse auction process is that you have to decide what you think a flight is worth. That's no easy task. Bid too low, and you'll just waste time as no-one will take you up on the offer. Bid too high and you run the risk of paying over the odds.

When you bid for a ticket you have to give your credit card details at the same time, so there's no changing your mind once your offer has been accepted. And although you enter the dates and times you want to travel when bidding, you won't necessarily get the time or date you want, so flexibility is required.

Priceline simply says that you must be prepared to leave at any time between 6am and 10pm for European destinations, and at any time day or night for worldwide destinations. Other restrictions include the inability to buy children's tickets using the service and the lack of choice over in-flight meals. Once you've made your bid Priceline promises to get back to you within an hour.

Another point to bear in mind is that Priceline doesn't check with the discount direct-selling airlines, such as easyJet, Ryanair and Go!, so compare prices with these as well.

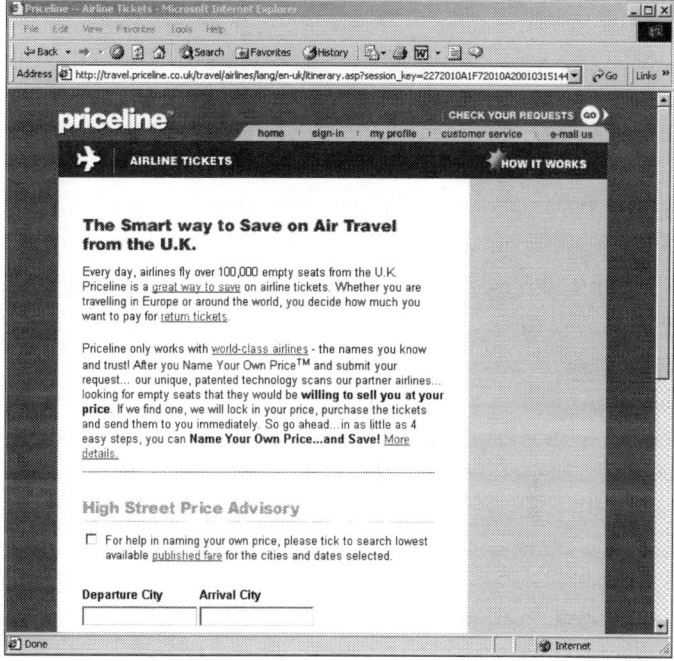

This reverse auction site (www.priceline.co.uk) allows browsers to set the price for a flight they require, which is then presented to the relevant airline to either accept or reject.

Other useful sites

Comparison shopping
Kelkoo (www.kelkoo.com)

European shopping agent and price comparison site Kelkoo has added a travel section to its site. Click on the 'Flights' section, enter your chosen destination and the dates you want to travel, and Kelkoo will trawl all the main online travel agents for the best deals. The service isn't perfect yet, but the concept is a winner. Even with the number of helpful online agents around, finding cheap flights is still a very complicated, and sometimes frustrating, business. Any online service that aims to make the process simpler has to be welcomed.

Scorecard (www.scorecard.com)

US company Gomez provides a whole range of ratings services, including one for online travel agents. Have a look to see which ones its rates most highly. At the moment the service is restricted to US sites.

Advice
Flying with Kids (www.flyingwithkids.com)

If you've ever flown with young children you'll know how stressful it can be. Take a look at this site for humourous advice on how to make the process as painless as possible.

Air Traveler's Handbook (www.cs.cmu.edu/afs/cs/user/ mkant/public/travel/airfare.html)

This is a list of frequently asked questions (FAQ) compiled from the **rec.travel.air** newsgroup. Everything you ever wanted to know about flight, and some things you didn't.

Instead of browsing through all the online travel agents yourself, log on to Kelkoo (www.kelkoo.com), state your travel requirements, and they will find the best deal currently available.

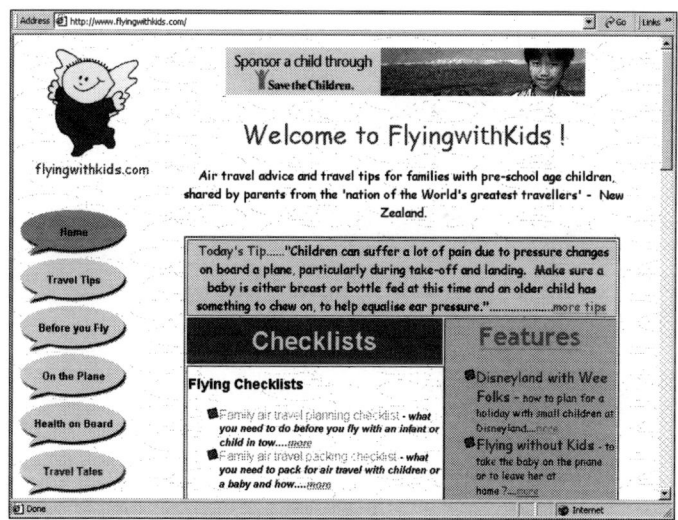

An informative website about flying with children (www.flyingwithkids.com), from important health matters to ideas for keeping them entertained.

Cheap fares checklist

1. First check the websites of the airline companies that fly to your destination. They may have time-limited special offers on certain destinations.

2. Compare this price with those offered by discount travel agents.

3. Then check the direct-selling discount airlines.

4. Also try the general online holiday agents, such as Bargainholidays.

5. You may strike it lucky with an auction site, such as QXL.

6. Find out the relevant airport taxes for your journey and make sure you know whether the quoted price includes these.

7. Take 40% from the cheapest fare you can find then make a bid on Priceline at this level. You've got nothing to lose and a bargain fare to gain. Bear in mind that Priceline bids are pre-tax and and they'll add a £5 handling charge on top.

Chapter 4

Accommodation

Introduction

The internet is helping us to put our impulsive desires for escape into action. 'Let's go away . . . anywhere . . . now!' A few clicks of the mouse and there are suggestions galore for places to escape to at home and abroad. Such are the advances in air travel that we can be in a European beauty spot within a couple of hours these days, lapping up the intoxicating aroma of a different culture.

In this chapter we look at booking hotels, bed & breakfasts, hostels and any other type of accommodation you can think of. Whether you fancy a long weekend in a chocolate-box cottage in the Cotswolds or a couple of nights in a romantic Parisian hotel, we give you the websites that can fulfil your desires most efficiently.

As with other travel services, accommodation is ideally suited to the web. Large amounts of complex data can be catalogued easily and interrogated online. Information can be updated speedily so you're sure of getting the very latest deals. International hotel chains can advertise their offerings far more efficiently. Local bed & breakfast establishments can reach a much wider audience on the web at much lower cost than advertising in brochures. And all these cost savings for the industry are trickling down to the consumer. You can achieve savings on room rates of up to 70% when you book online sometimes. Even major hotel chains are offering internet-only room rates.

There are hundreds of accommodation-related websites out there. We've selected just some of the best that can save you time and money.

Hotel chains

Some people become unshakably attached to a particular hotel chain once they've had a pleasant experience in one of its establishments. If finding the right sort of hotel is more important to you than finding the cheapest roof over your head, go straight to the hotel chain website and book from there. Most major chains have now introduced online booking, with some offering discounts to encourage you to use the service.

> **TIP**
>
> *Even major hotel chains are offering internet-only room rates.*

International chains

Hilton Hotels	**www.hilton.com**
Sheraton	**www.sheraton.com**
Holiday Inn	**www.holiday-inn.com**
Radisson Hotels	**www.radisson.com**
Crowne Plaza	**www.basshotels.com/ crowneplaza**
Four Seasons	**www.fourseasons.com**
Hyatt	**www.hyatt.com**

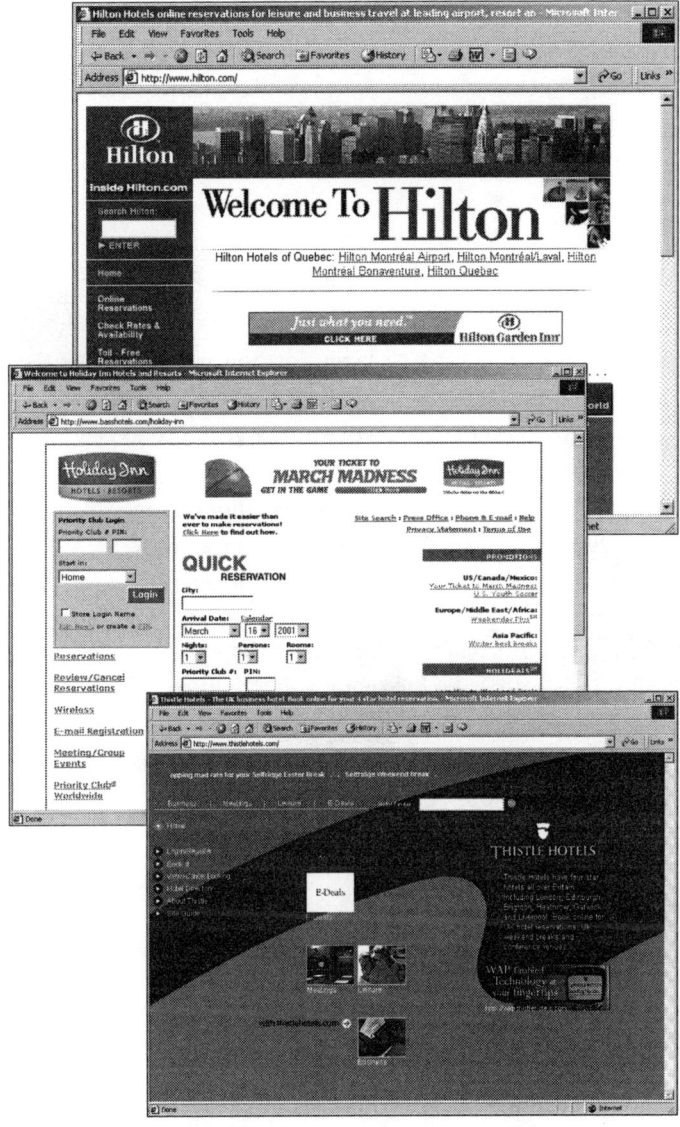

Many of the major hotel chains now have websites detailing their accommodation facilities and online booking, from the luxury (www.hilton.com), to more standard chain hotels (www.holiday-inn.com), to national chains, such as the UK's Thistle group (www.thistlehotels.com).

Inter-Continental	www.interconti.com
Le Méridien	www.lemeridien-hotels.com
Mandarin Oriental	www.mandarin-oriental.com
Accor	www.accor.com
Marriott International	www.marriott.com

UK chains

Britannia	www.britanniahotels.com
Moat House Hotels	www.moathousehotels.co.uk
Posthouse	www.posthouse-hotels.co.uk
Jarvis	www.jarvis.co.uk
The Savoy Group	www.savoy-group.co.uk
Swallow Hotels	www.swallowhotels.com
Thistle	www.thistlehotels.com
Travelodge	www.travelodge.co.uk
Travelinn	www.travelinn.co.uk

Bear in mind that many of the hotel groups own several chains. If you can't see the brand you like listed, look for it using the excellent DMOZ directory: **DMOZ Open Directory Project** (www.dmoz.org/Recreation/Travel/Reservations/ Lodging/Hotels/Hotel_Chains)

Hotel finders

These websites attempt to provide an all-round accommodation service, finding you somewhere to stay at hundreds of hotels, B&Bs and hostels around the world. There isn't one service that covers absolutely everything – yet. As ever, you will have to try several to get a feel for what's out there in the area you want to stay and at the price you can afford.

International

Hotel Guide (www.hotelguide.com)

Switzerland-based Hotel Guide offers a database of more than 60,000 hotels in 200 countries worldwide. The website is searchable in seven languages, and you can access the database via WAP-enabled mobile phone **(http://wap.hotel guide.com)**, too. Just search on a town or city and the list of available hotels comes up with links to pictures, ratings and reviews, plus website links and room rates. You can book online and there are often discounts of 10% or more. The room rates are given in the local currency but there is a currency converter on the website. It would be better if these conversions were done automatically and included in the hotel list, but the site is an excellent resource nonetheless.

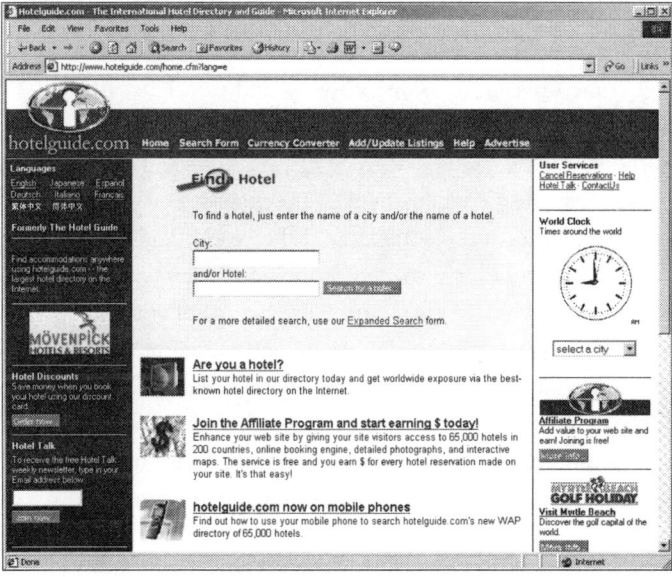

One of the most comprehensive of all the hotel-finding websites is the Hotel Guide (www.hotelguide.com), covering accommodation all over the world.

Accommodation Search Engine (www.ase.net)

This is a massive directory of more than 140,000 international accommodation web-pages from all over the world. You can search by price range, accommodation type, amenities and facility requirements. You can also save information on your favourite hotels, write reviews and share them with friends. The room rates are quoted in the currency of your choice and you can visit the hotels' websites and book online.

Places To Stay (www.placestostay.com)

This is the consumer-facing website of hotel database company **WorldRes** (www.worldres.com), which hires out its reservation system to around 900 other websites, including the UK's largest internet service provider, **Freeserve** (http://freeserve.worldres.com/index.html). So the chances are that a large number of hotel finder websites you visit will come up with the same answers and prices because they'll be powered by WorldRes. It makes sense to go to the source.

The database contains over 17,000 hotels, bed & breakfasts, inns and resorts around the world, including smaller, independently owned properties it claims you won't find anywhere else. WorldRes also maintains that its reservation system is more efficient, and therefore cheaper, than the traditional Global Distribution System used by most of the industry. The database is certainly user-friendly, with lots of different ways of searching, and there are usually accompanying pictures of the accommodation, too.

Hotelstravel.com (www.hotelstravel.com)

This site boasts over 75,000 links to lodging and travel resources worldwide, including all the hotel chains you could possibly think of. Sites are categorised by country to make international travel planning a doddle.

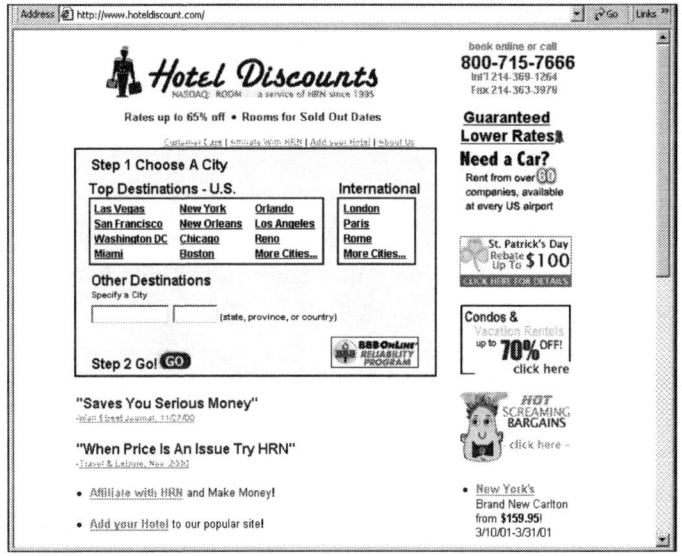

This very useful website for travellers to the US offers substantially discounted accommodation in all the major cities (www.hoteldiscount.com).

Hotel Discounts (www.hoteldiscount.com)

If you're going to the USA, Hotel Discount, from the Hotel Reservations Network, promises discounts of up to 70% on a wide selection of major US cities and a more restricted selection of European destinations. You can book online or by phone and there's a helpful currency converter, too.

ClickAndGoNow (www.clickandgonow.com)

This claims to be Europe's largest online hotel booking service, offering 'up to 60%' off normal room rates in over 7,000 hotels. The company reckons that by December 2001 it will be processing 100,000 bookings per month for rooms in over 50,000 hotels. It has an interesting special offers section and all the usual international search and online booking facilities. It even lets you know the room availability status of each hotel. The only drawback is that there's no currency converter.

Laterooms (www.laterooms.com)

Late Rooms is an excellent international hotel database that aims to cut out the middleman by allowing hotels to advertise their available rooms directly on the website. It promises discounts of up to 75% on the normal room rates and prices quoted are per room, not per person. The site includes helpful information on the accommodation providers listed, plus links to their websites if they have them. The only drawback is the lack of photographs to accompany the information, but at least more and more hotels do seem to be setting up their own websites with pictures and more detailed information. You also have to book by telephone.

Lastminute.com (www.lastminute.com)

Rather than providing a comprehensive hotel directory, Lastminute concentrates on discount deals and special offers categorised regionally. There's also a budget section for

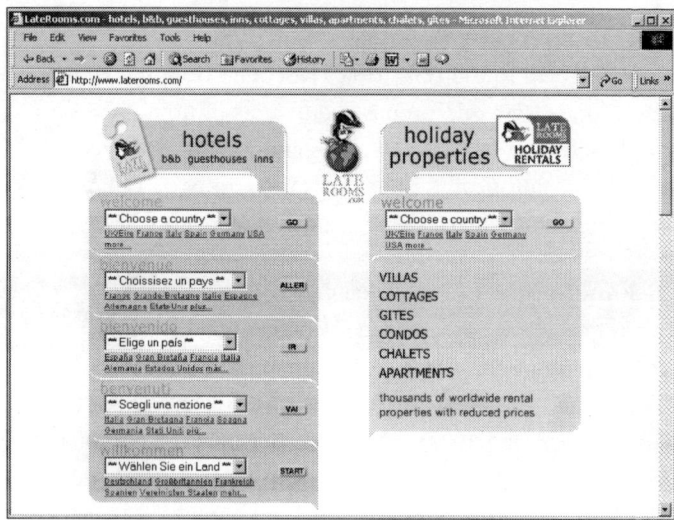

Ideal for last-minute holidays, this website (www.laterooms.com) details up-to-date availability and good discounts from hotels hoping to fill empty rooms at short notice.

accommodation costing £50 and under per night. If you don't mind particularly where you stay, you could pick up some interesting bargains here.

Need A Hotel (www.needahotel.com)

Offers 10,000 hotels in 80 countries worldwide, including every destination flown to by discount airline Ryanair. The two companies have a strategic partnership. You can obtain 10% discounts if you book through the site.

All Hotels (www.all-hotels.com)

Over 60,000 hotels are on offer via this comprehensive Edinburgh-based site. It has aggregated several other online databases, so there may be some overlap with sites already mentioned. The booking procedure allows you to record your preferences for future use. There are several helpful accommodation categories, from international hotels to budget bargains, and searches by area can be very specific.

Hotel World Guide (www.hotelworld.com)

This well-organised site contains details of around 9,000 hotels in 204 countries. You can book online with all of them and receive instant confirmation.

Hotelnet (www.hotelnet.co.uk)

Hotelnet is another international hotel directory, part of Holidaybreak plc, with 9,000 hotels on offer. It specialises in affiliations with leading hotel chain brands, such as Forte, Marriott and Hilton, and many of the smaller chains, too. Some of the hotels featured offer real-time confirmation of bookings.

Holiday-Rentals.com (www.holiday-rentals.co.uk)

If you want to rent on a self-catering basis, Holiday Rentals has a selection of 3,500 properties worldwide. Photos of each

Cosy living room

A well-illustrated website that details self-catering options all over the world, including interior and exterior property views so nothing should come as a surprise (www.holiday-rentals.co.uk).

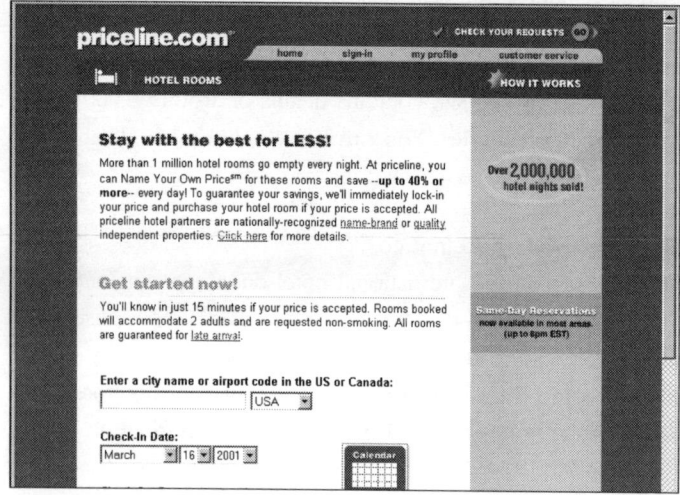

This reverse auction site (www.priceline.com) allows you to quote a nightly room price at a chosen hotel, which the said hotel then has the option to accept or reject. Great discounts, as hotels are often keen to fill empty rooms.

house are provided, and links to other tourist or travel sites help with planning a trip. Booking can be done online, and there is also a selection of golf and skiing holidays.

Priceline (www.priceline.com)

Priceline is a US company offering reverse auction facilities to consumers, whereby you say how much you are prepared to pay for a room and the accommodation provider decides whether or not to accept your offer. Priceline estimates that one million hotel rooms go empty every night – rooms that hotels would like to see filled, even if it means discounting them by up to 40%. Just key in the dates and city where you want to stay, the hotel quality level, and the price you want to pay per night. The dynamic search engine advises you if it thinks your offer price is so low that it has little chance of being accepted. If your price is accepted, Priceline books the rooms using the credit card details you provide. Priceline promises to let you know whether your offer has been accepted within 15 minutes.

UK-specific

Most of the hotel-finder sites above contain UK-specific sections, as do the online travel agents mentioned in **Holidays** (*see page 91*). But there are a number of UK specialist sites that go into more depth. Here are some of the best.

The AA Hotel Guide

(http://www.theaa.com/getaway/hotels/hotels_home.jsp)
If you like the idea of the place you stay at being carefully vetted and approved by experts in the field, you'll be happy using the AA's hotel guide. It lists around 8,000 establishments in the UK and Ireland, each one regularly inspected and rated according to the AA's rigorous quality standards. You can search on a number of criteria, from

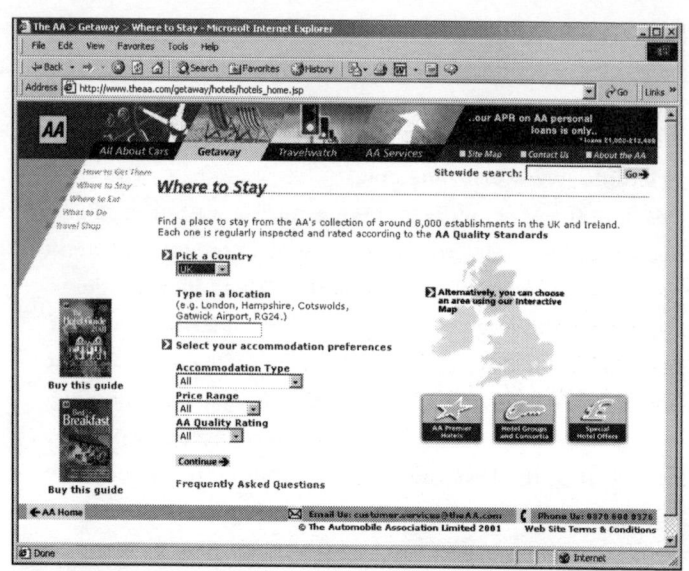

The Getaway section of the AA's website (www.theaa.com) offers a hotel search with a fair guarantee of quality, given the association's strict rating system.

accommodation type to price. You can also sort the results in any way you want. Gastronomes may prefer to sort the results according to food quality, for example. You can book online once you've registered.

A2Btravel (www.a2btravel.com/accommodation.html)

The UK section of A2Btravel's accommodation section contains over 33,000 hotels, bed & breakfasts and inns. The search engine is very detailed, allowing you to narrow down your search to places that offer gym and leisure facilities, for example. There are no ratings guides, though.

Hotelmaster (www.hotelmaster.co.uk)

Hotelmaster offers over 35,000 places to stay in Britain, although the information about the hotels and guesthouses is

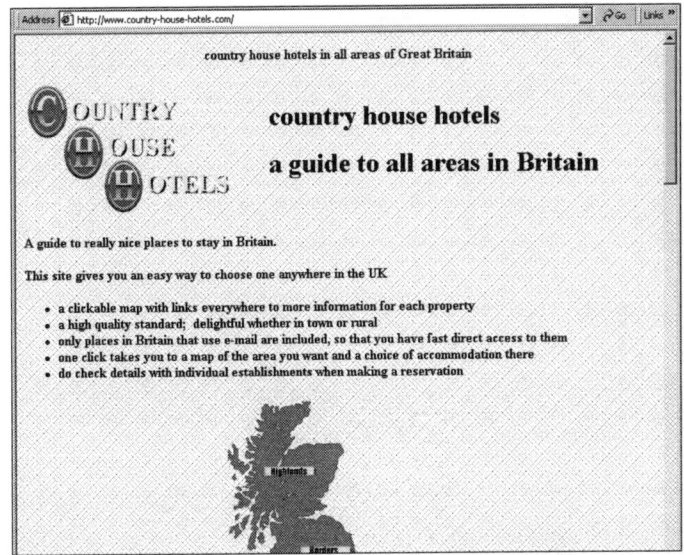

Address http://www.country-house-hotels.com/

country house hotels in all areas of Great Britain

country house hotels
a guide to all areas in Britain

A guide to really nice places to stay in Britain.

This site gives you an easy way to choose one anywhere in the UK

- a clickable map with links everywhere to more information for each property
- a high quality standard; delightful whether in town or rural
- only places in Britain that use e-mail are included, so that you have fast direct access to them
- one click takes you to a map of the area you want and a choice of accommodation there
- do check details with individual establishments when making a reservation

A useful link to some of the finest and most picturesque country hotels in Britain, easily located via a nationwide map (www.country-house-hotels.com).

rather sparse and there's no online booking function. But there are accompanying maps to let you know exactly where you'll be staying.

Country House Hotels (www.country-house-hotels.com)
'A guide to really nice places to stay in Britain.' So says the website. If quality and quaintness is more important than price, this site gives you a reasonable selection of interesting hotels in Britain. There's no online booking facility, though.

B&B My Guest (www.beduk.co.uk)
A simple pun and a simple website offering 300 B&Bs throughout Britain. There are clear photos of the establishments and you can book online.

Tucked Up (www.tuckedup.com)

This is a promising-looking site from KGP Publishing, which features B&B and self-catering directories, plus a rapidly developing hotels section. There are over 1,000 UK B&Bs listed here, organised by county. Most have pictures and you can book online. The self-catering section features over 600 properties, from castles to coach houses.

Fairhaven Holiday Cottages (www.fairhaven-holidays.co.uk)

Specialist in self-catering accommodation in the UK for long weekends and extended breaks.

English Country Cottages (www.english-country-cottages.co.uk)

This self-explanatory site offers over 3,000 properties throughout England, Scotland and Wales. You can't book online, but you can check prices and availability. Booking is by e-mail or telephone.

Internet Cottages (www.internet-cottages.com)

A neat and simple site listing more country cottages for rent. The pictures are clear and booking is via e-mail or phone direct with the owners.

The National Trust Cottages (www.nationaltrust.org.uk/cottages)

If spectacular scenery and places of historical interest are your scene, the National Trust's collection of holiday cottages is worth a look. It has nearly 300 cottages, houses and apartments on offer, from Cornish fishermen's cottages to apartments in the heart of our historic cities. You can order the full colour brochure online and there are some late-booking special offers, but no online booking facility.

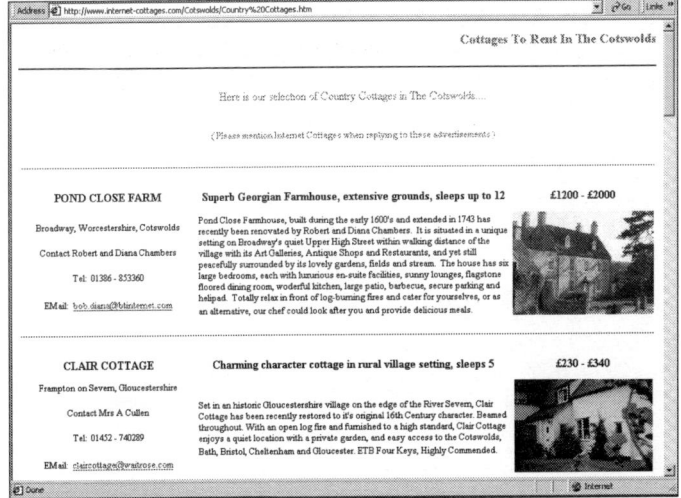

For lovers of self-catering holidays, this well-illustrated website offers country cottages to rent in a range of sizes and prices (www.internet-cottages.com).

Pets On Holiday (www.pets-on-holiday.com)

Animal-lovers will find this site extremely useful. It simply lists accommodation that welcomes animals. Enough said.

Hostels

A t the budget end of the scale, hostels can provide cheap, reasonable accommodation for travellers more interested in a good night's sleep than the merits of the minibar.

Hostels.com (www.hostels.com)

Hostels.com, headquartered in San Francisco, USA, boasts the largest database of hostels in the world. The site is an all-round must for the budding backpacker, with links galore and community pages for travellers to share tips and tales. Many of the hostels are now bookable online, too.

Despite its name, the youth hostel association offers a range of economy accommodation options for all ages, all of which are detailed on their website (www.yha.org.uk).

Youth Hostels Association (www.yha.org.uk)

The YHA has sloughed its bobble-hat image and now has a slick website listing over 250 hostels in England and Wales, 100 of which are bookable online. And many are not just for youths either – families are welcome at over 100. You can book family bunk-bed rooms for under £50 a night.

Camping and caravanning

For those who really want to get close to nature, tents and caravans are the only form of accommodation worth bothering with. Try these sites for places to pitch up and boil the billycan:

European Camping Index	**www.oginet.com/camping**
USA Camp Sites	**www.usacampsites.com**
Eurocamp	**www.eurocamp.co.uk**

Lovers of the outdoors will find a range of websites detailing camping and caravanning options around the world, including Europe- (www.oginet.com /camping) and UK-specific sites (www.camping.uk-directory.com).

Keycamp	**www.keycamp.co.uk**
Camping France	**www.campingfrance.co.uk**
UK Camping and	**www.camping.uk-**
Caravanning Directory	**directory.com**
Caravan SiteFinder UK	**www.caravan-sitefinder.co.uk**

Home exchange

One unusual, but increasingly popular, way of organising a holiday on the cheap without necessarily compromising on the level of accommodation, is home exchange. Basically, you swap houses for a few weeks with people who want to come to your country. You get to stay for free in – hopefully – an interesting and characterful property with none of the artificiality and superficiality associated with some bland hotels. You're more likely to be based in the heart of a community rather than banished to some roundabout at the edge of a city's ring road.

You obviously have to feel you can trust the people you loan your own house to, and there are insurance considerations to take into account. This level of trust takes time to build up and is usually established through regular communication by e-mail or phone. Home exchange websites resemble communities of like-minded people for this reason. With most sites you have to become a member.

Clearly, it's wise to be truthful about the size and quality of your property and honest about the merits of the area you live in, otherwise you could end up with some very disgruntled holidaymakers. And if you get a reputation for being 'economical with the actualité' you could find yourself being barred from home exchange websites. When you list the details of your property you also say where you would prefer to go to stay. But the fun of home exchange is that you may receive an offer from someone living in a place you'd never thought of going. It can broaden your horizons.

The websites act as agents bringing interested parties together. You advertise your property online (typical cost £20), including pictures where possible, and peruse the adverts left by other home exchangers. The system works particularly well for families wanting to travel long distances,

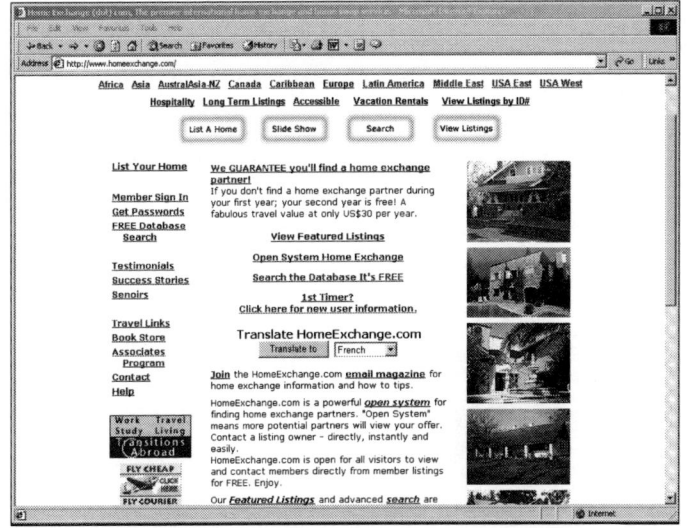

If you fancy a more homespun experience while travelling, home exchange sites such as this one (www.homexchange.com) list properties all over the world which the owners are prepared to "swap" with yours for a holiday period.

where a 100% saving on the accommodation could make a big difference to the total cost of the holiday.

Here are some leading home exchange sites to check out:

International Home Exchange Network	**www.homexchange.com**
Homelink International	**www.homelink.org.uk**
Holi-Swaps	**www.holiswaps.com**
Home Exchange Vacations	**www.homebase-hols.com**
Latitudes Home Exchange	**www.home-swap.com**

Chapter 5

Car Rental

Introduction

Renting a car whilst on a trip or on holiday is yet another piece in the complex jigsaw of travel planning. There are so many other elements to think about that this one, like foreign currency, can often get lost in the mix. Car rental may sound straightforward, but it can be tricky. You have to know exactly where and when you want to pick up the car and where and when you'll return it. Not all companies will allow you to return the car to a different location, or to a location that suits you, rather than direct to the rental company.

Luckily, the web is making it easier to plan journeys and book cars in locations all round the world. Most of the major rental companies now offer booking online, and almost all the holiday agent websites include a car rental section. The beauty of using an online agent is that it can do all the shopping around for you and hopefully find you the best price.

The two main variables that affect the daily price of a rental car are its size/specification, and the time of year you want it. When demand is high during the holiday season, prices inevitably go up. Another point to bear in mind is that insurance policies can vary markedly from company to company. You may be getting a cheap daily rate, but check the smallprint to see what level of excess you have to pay in the event of any claim. Speaking from experience, a cracked windscreen can end up doubling the amount you pay for a week's rental. Also check for exclusions and other conditions, such as excess mileage penalties.

Car rental companies

Avis Car Rental (www.avis.com)

One of the leading car rental companies has a well-organised site, allowing you to book online, amend or cancel reservations, for both business and personal use. You can browse through the fleet to find the country and car of your choice. There are also links to hotel and airline sites through 'Avis Travel Partners'. Existing Avis customers can access a fast-track method of booking online using a unique membership number.

> **WARNING**
>
> *Insurance policies can vary markedly from company to company. Remember to check the smallprint.*

Hertz Car Rental (www.hertz.com)

The giant amongst car rental companies, Hertz offers everything you need to hire a car in most parts of the world. But, as with many market leaders, you won't necessarily find the cheapest prices. They didn't get rich by being at the discount end of the market. Until recently, these happy few had the car rental market sewn up. Thankfully more competitors have since entered the fray, bringing some welcome price pressures on to the incumbents. Having said

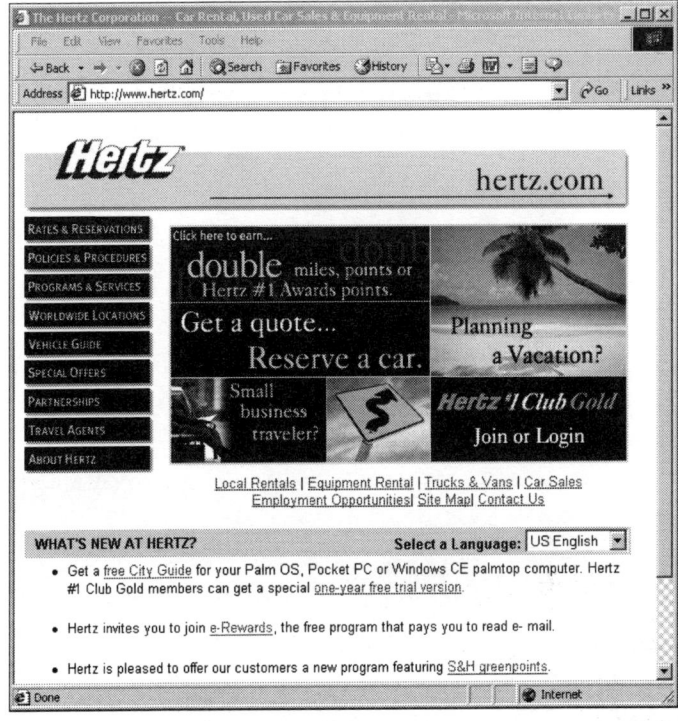

One of the world's largest car rental firms has a comprehensive website (www.hertz.com) which includes discounts and special offers when renting online.

that, there's a lot to be said for paying more in return for reliability and efficiency. Regular users receive special rates, but there's also a special deals section for bargain hunters. The online application process is thorough, giving you the option to select baby seats, for example, or to choose a car that is equipped to carry skis. The quotations can be converted into the currency of your choice.

Europcar (www.europcar.com)

Despite its name, Europcar operates in 100 countries and 2,400 locations worldwide, including recently added Australia.

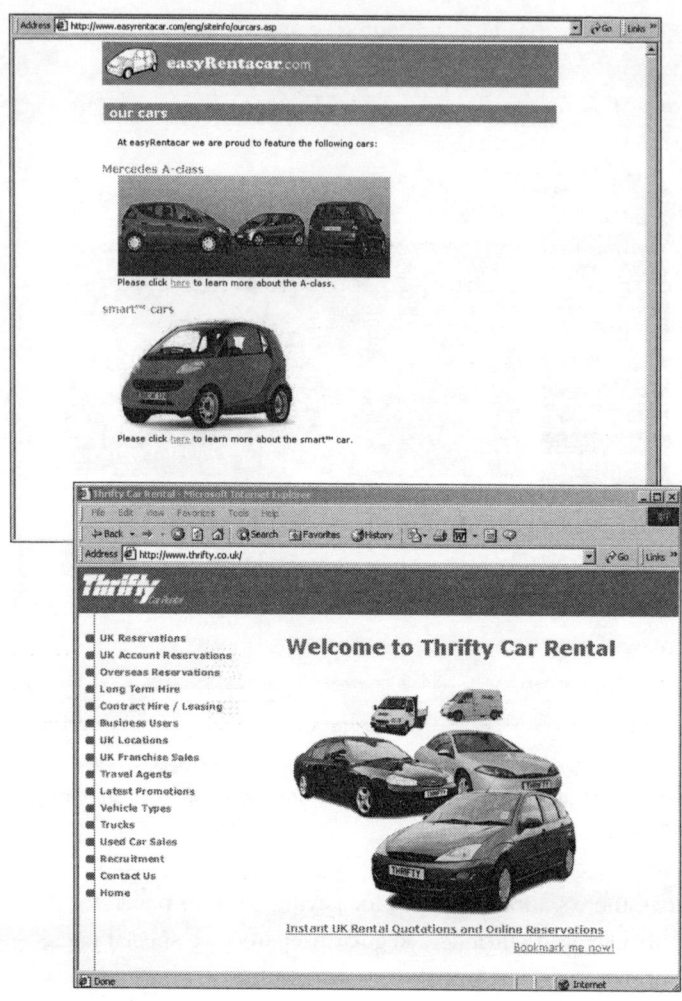

Websites catering to the cheaper end of the market include easyRentacar (top, www.easyrentacar.com) and Thrifty (bottom, www.thrifty.co.uk).

Its main site has links through to country-specific sites that list various special offers for internet customers. Although you can book online, the reservation system is very fiddly and sometimes frustrating.

Thrifty Car Rentals (www.thrifty.co.uk)

Thrifty offers both international and UK rental promising instant online quotations and booking. There are cars in over 1,200 locations throughout 55 countries. Some overseas locations require a credit card number before they quote. The quotation system is quick and easy to use, and the quoted rates apply only to online reservations.

easyRentacar (www.easyrentacar.com)

This is an internet-only car rental company in the same group as the easyJet airline. It displays the same no-frills, cut price approach to the job. Prices are quoted on a daily basis and are different depending on which day of the week you want to rent the car. Once you've asked for a quote, you can amend it by selecting other cheaper days, or deselecting the more expensive ones. Once you've made a booking you can't cancel it and get a refund. At the moment easyRentacar's locations are restricted to major European cities, but it does have plans to roll out its service further. This is one site where you have to watch the conditions like a hawk – there are lots of them, so make sure you don't get caught out.

Budget Rent-A-Car (www.drivebudget.com)

This is the third-largest rental group in the world, offering cars in 3,000 locations around the world. Despite this, it does have the feel of a primarily US site – only US residents can book online, for example. There are internet-only rates and special offers galore.

Comparison services

Travelocity (www.travelocity.co.uk)

The all-round travel site owned by Sabre has an excellent car rental section. Just fill in the online form giving details of where and when you want to pick up the car, and it scouts round for the cheapest prices. You can either choose a specific rental company, or compare prices offered by Travelocity's 'Featured Partners' – Advantage, Alamo, Avis, Budget, Dollar, Enterprise, Hertz, National, Payless, and Thrifty. Travelocity says its partners offer special rates and instant confirmation at the time of reservation. But you can widen the search even more to cover over 50 car rental companies on its database.

Holiday Autos (www.holidayautos.co.uk)

This is a truly excellent broker service because of its simplicity and good design. It makes choosing and booking a car child's play. It offers 750,000 cars in over 4,000 locations worldwide. Prices are fully inclusive and seem competitive, plus there's a £5 discount for online bookings. There is also a useful late-booking section for bargain-hunting travellers. The service is aimed at holidaymakers, rather than business people. Interesting innovations include 'no insurance excess' deals and price guarantees. No wonder it is used by several of the leading online travel agents.

Rentadeal.com (www.rentadeal.com)

This company is primarily focused on the USA, but there are some worldwide locations to choose from. Rentadeal promises savings of up to 30% by shopping around its large panel of rental companies on your behalf.

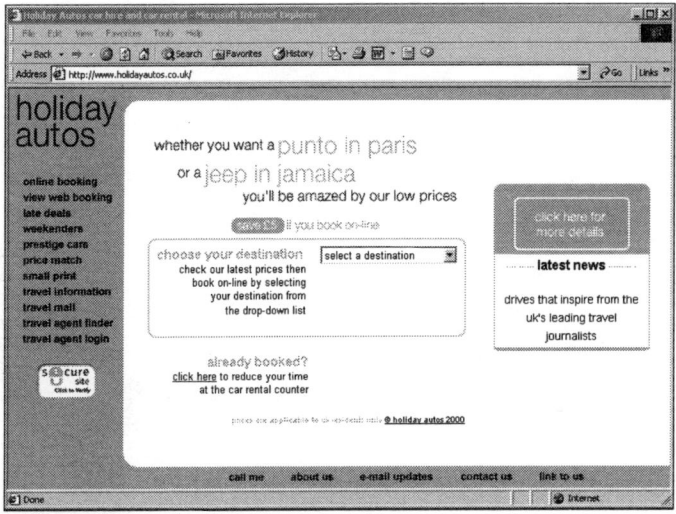

One of the most reasonable and well organised of all the car rental websites (www.holidayautos.co.uk), the site includes online discounts and various other special deals.

Ebookers (www.ebookers.com/travelagent/cars)

An all-round travel booking site that has an impressive car rental section with the usual search engine that throws up the cheapest prices from a panel of rental companies. The prices for each category of car are clearly displayed and booking online is a straightforward step-by-step process.

Chapter 6

Holidays

Introduction

Anyone new to the web may be overwhelmed by the sheer number of holiday-related websites that have sprung up. It seems that the whole industry has moved online, from tour operators to travel agents. The web is an incredibly useful interactive medium for companies and holidaymakers alike. We can search through hundreds of holiday ideas online far more easily than through conventional catalogues and brochures. Information can be sorted in a variety of ways that makes price and quality comparisons a cinch. As confidence grows in the web as a secure medium, more people are booking online using their credit and debit cards, and more holiday companies are offering secure online booking facilities.

Categorizing all these sites is difficult given that many attempt to be all things to all people, including all types of holiday and all types of travel-related service on their sites. Other sites stick to what they think they're good at, whether that's skiing holidays or cruises. As ever, you'll have to peruse quite a few sites to find your ideal holiday, but daydreaming about escape to sunnier climes doesn't seem to be the most onerous of chores. The more flexible you are prepared to be with your destination and time of travel, the more likely it is you'll find a bargain.

Tour operators and holiday companies

The Association of Independent Tour Operators (www.aito.co.uk)

This is as good a place to start as any. AITO represents over 160 independent and specialist tour operators in the UK and has set up a website to market their holidays and short breaks. You can search for holidays by activity or country, and there are sections for late availability bargains and special

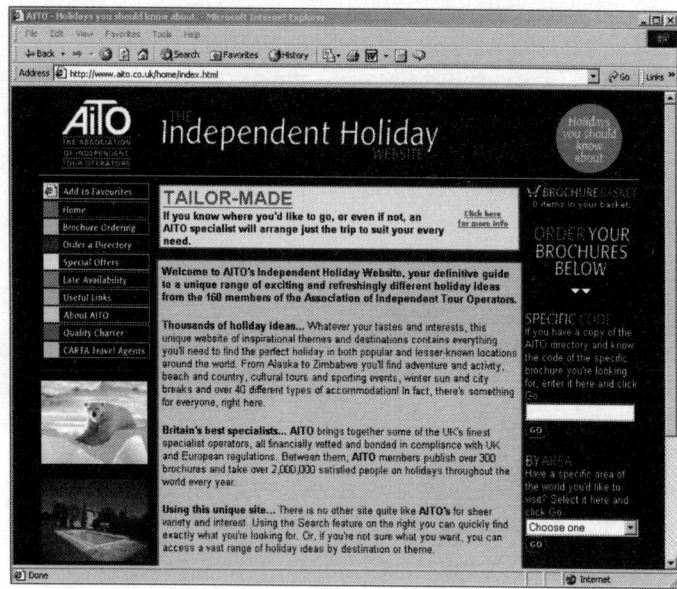

If you're not sure which travel agent to approach, or what kind of holiday you would prefer, AITO's portal website links you to any tour operator that matches your given criteria (www.aito.co.uk).

offers. You can also order brochures online and look for a local affiliated travel agent in your area if a bricks-and-mortar presence still appeals.

Airtours (www.airtours.com)

This travel group seems to own everything, from airlines to camping holiday operators. The group website gives links to all the holiday companies it owns, including big names such as Going Places (*see page 95*), Saga, and Airtours Holidays. It also owns Late Escapes, the holiday auction website (*see page 115*). Not all of its companies offer online brochures and booking, though.

Thomson Holidays (www.thomson-holidays.com)

The UK's largest holiday company offers a comprehensive website full of different types of holiday, from luxury cruises to last-minute package deals. The site is searchable in a number of ways. You can simply select the country you want to visit, or browse some of its specialist holidays, from deluxe to cut-price. Its no-frills holiday brand **Just (www.just.co.uk)** is bookable online, but you have to ring to book most of the other holidays.

JMC (www.holidays.jmc.com)

Owned by travel agent Thomas Cook, JMC is trying to simplify the holiday by breaking it up into its constituent parts. So you can book flights only as well as package holidays to the sun. The site is trendy in its design and the search engine logical and straightforward.

First Choice (www.firstchoiceholidaysplc.com)

One of the 'big four' UK holiday groups with fingers in most pies – an airline, travel agents, and tour operators. Its long list of tour operators includes First Choice Holidays and Unijet, whilst its main travel agent is Travelchoice (*see page 104*).

Travel agents

Thomas Cook (www.thomascook.com)

A lot of people still believe that brand recognition is more important than price. Bitter experience has taught such people that you tend to get what you pay for in life. So they conclude that it's worth paying a little bit more in return for peace of mind. This is precisely the attitude that the likes of Thomas Cook have been attempting to foster with their multimillion-pound advertising campaigns over the years. So don't expect to find the cheapest holidays, but if you want a one-stop-shop holiday site for a hassle-free booking experience, this is up your street. You can book flights, sun and snow holidays, plus the obligatory last-minute deals from other tour operators as well as its own JMC.

On top of this, you can also order foreign currency and traveller's cheques online and have the money delivered to

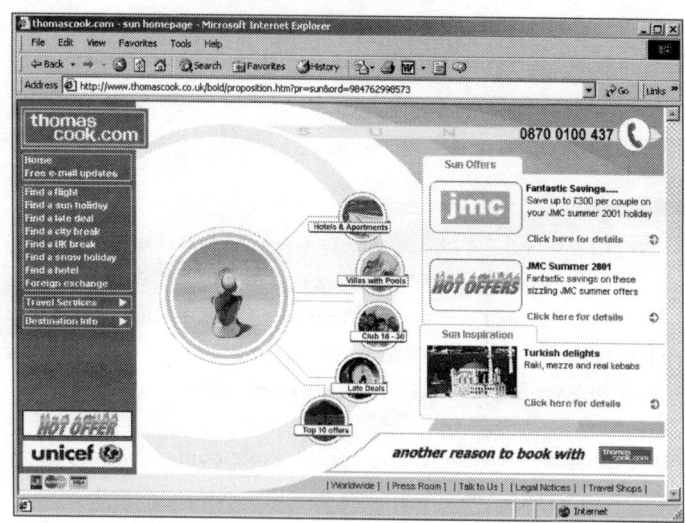

Not surprising for one of the world's largest and oldest travel companies, Thomas Cook's website (www.thomascook.com) offers everything you could need for booking a holiday online, from package deals to insurance.

your door for £5. Although Thomas Cook doesn't charge commission you're not necessarily guaranteed to get the best exchange rate around. Similarly with its online travel insurance quotation service. But again, those booking through Thomas Cook probably won't mind a paying a bit extra here and there for the sake of convenience.

Lunn Poly (www.lunnpoly.com)
Browse through Lunn Poly's brochures online, categorised according to the type of holiday activity, and check its last-minute deals, too. Don't expect much by way of interactivity though – bookings are by phone.

Going Places (www.going-places.co.uk)
This Airtours-owned travel agent specialises in late deals and a holiday-planning service it calls Matchmaker. The 'Search and Match' facility recommends resorts and properties and checks availability. You can also book car hire, overnight hotel stays, and even sort out hotel parking. The site is nattily designed using Flash animation software, although there could be more information about the company itself and what it does and booking is by phone only.

Realholiday (www.realholiday.co.uk)
This is a site created by the Campaign for Real Travel Agents, an organisation dedicated to fighting the consolidation within the travel industry that has seen just four holiday groups take over airlines, tour operators and travel agents. Some see this as bad for choice. CARTA members are all independent of the major travel groups and promise to offer holidays that are a bit different from your run-of-the-mill package tour to the Balearics. Realholiday has its own range of exclusive holidays culled from its members and links to member websites, too. CARTA is closely allied to Association of Independent Tour Operators (*see page 92*).

Online travel agents: top, www.realholiday.co.uk; centre, www.otcuk.com; and bottom, www.escaperoutes.com.

A2Btravel.com (www.a2btravel.com)

This is the daddy of the online travel agents, simply bursting with holidays and travel-related services of all kinds. Whether you want to book a spur-of-the-moment run to the sun or a self-catering villa in Tuscany, A2B can offer something. It aggregates holidays from a wide range of travel companies. For example, its last-minute bargains are actually supplied by **Bargainholidays** (*see page 103*).

Online Travel Company (www.otcuk.com)

This Twickenham-based company has a 150-strong customer support staff behind its internet façade, so don't let the 'dot com' bit put you off. OTC offers its own package deals plus last-minute bargains from other holiday companies, too. You can also arrange all the other usual elements of travel, such as car hire and travel insurance.

The First Resort (www.firstresort.com)

This is a package holiday aggregator site part-owned by Thomson Holidays, one of the UK's largest tour operators. Despite this, it promises to be impartial and not plug its own holidays, but it does stick to the major brand names, so don't expect too much in the way of exotic, specialist holidays. It also promises to undercut your high-street bucket shop price by £20 and, if you register, it will send you an e-mail newsletter detailing the all the latest special offers, including last-minute deals.

Holiday Bank (www.holidaybank.co.uk)

If you particularly like staying in villas, cottages and chalets then Holiday Bank is the site for you. It offers thousands of holiday ideas at destinations around the world. It also has a section on activity holidays, from golf to painting.

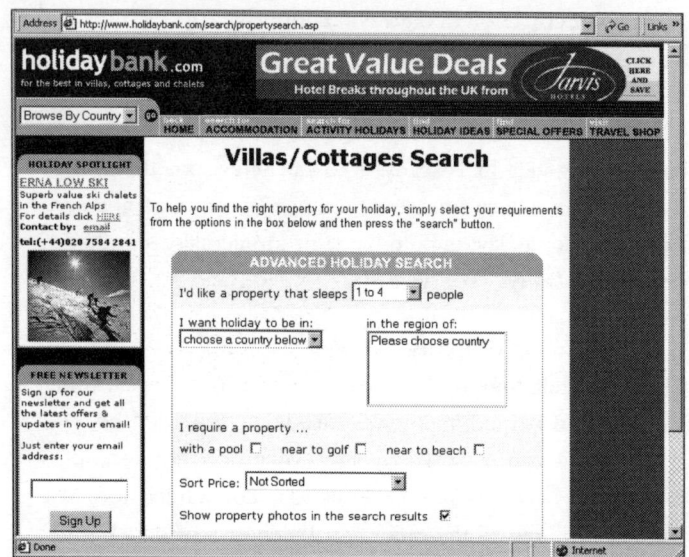

Self-catering holidays, from villas in the sun or winter country cottages, can be found through the straightforward search facility at Holiday Bank (www.holidaybank.com)

The Independent Traveller (www.independenttraveller.co.uk)

The very antithesis of the package holiday mentality, Independent Traveller is designed for the discerning holidaymaker who wants every element of a holiday to be just right, without compromise. You fill in a profile, detailing your requirements, and the company suggests the best way to fulfil your desires. It also offers a range of its own holidays and tours.

Escape Routes (www.escaperoutes.com)

This exceptionally well-laid-out site is another in the EMAP publishing empire stable, along with A2Btravel and 1Ski.com. It is, in fact, an online version of a holiday magazine of the same name. Flights, city breaks, holidays – this site seems to have it all (except online booking).

If you like the security of a tour operator but the freedom of movement when abroad, the Independent Traveller website (www.independent traveller.co.uk) can find a holiday to suit your requirements, from weekend breaks to long-haul.

Holiday Shopping Guide (www.holiday.beeb.com)

The commercial relation to the BBC's **Holiday** programme is a comprehensive resource for planning and booking holidays, including those featured in the show. You can also book flights and browse the many links to useful travel-related websites, including a range of partner online travel agents.

A1 Flights and Holidays (www.a1fah.co.uk)

A1 reckons it can offer up to 30% off normal package holiday deals by giving travellers more flexibility over the arrangements.

STA Travel (www.statravel.co.uk)

Students and those under 26 can pick up some amazing bargains at this specialist travel agent. It has over 250

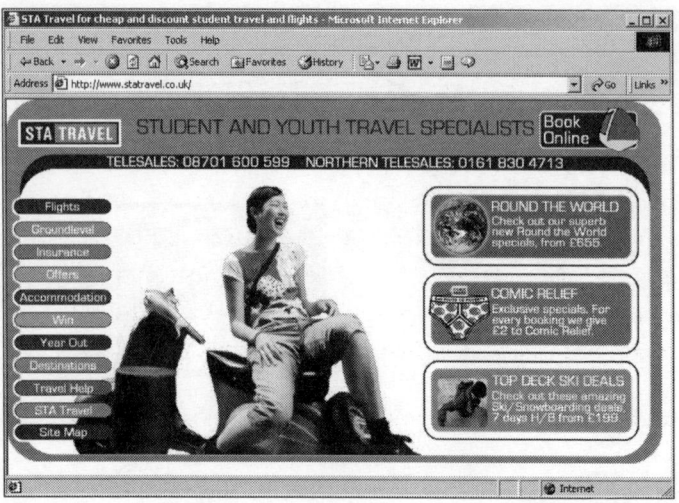

STA Travel (www.statravel.co.uk) specialises in discounted flights and holidays for travellers under the age of 26, and benefits from subsidiary branches all over the world.

branches worldwide. The site includes sections on cheap flights, package holidays and insurance, with plenty of advice for the young traveller. Essential viewing for the student taking a year out.

Teletext (www.teletext.co.uk)

It may be confusing to go to the website of a TV information service, but the fact is, Teletext does have lots of flight and holiday offers on its system, including late-availability bargains. You can save holiday details in a file for later, but there's no online booking, just links to the holiday operator.

Expedia (www.expedia.co.uk)

This all-round travel aggregator defines its 'Late Deals' as holidays with departure dates within the next ten weeks. Not as last-minute as some. There's also a general holidays section with 70,000 deals from 20 tour operators to choose from. Just

type in where and when you want to go, and up pop hordes
of holiday offers. Delve further and more details are given,
then you can book online there and then.

Ebookers (www.ebookers.com)
Ebookers is apparently Europe's most popular online travel
agent. Like Expedia, it offers the whole gamut of travel
services, from flights to travel insurance. Its holiday offerings
include package deals, specialist activity holidays, and city
breaks. You can book online or by phone with relative ease.

Holiday Rentals (www.holiday-rentals.co.uk)
Here, over 2,500 holiday cottages and villas are offered by
private individuals rather than holiday companies and hotel
chains. There are some wonderful bargains on offer,
especially in low season.

Last-minute bargain specialists

If you're footloose and fancy free and ready to pack
your bags at the drop of a hat, there are some great last-
minute holiday deals available on the web. Your place in
the sun is just a few mouse-clicks away . . . and a telephone
call, usually.

The last-minute bargain hunter shouldn't be too picky
about destination or accommodation. One thing websites
seldom show you is what your hotel or apartment looks like.
In fact, the lack of accommodation photos is a serious failing
on many of the package holiday travel sites. And bear in
mind that with some very late bookings, you're not even
allocated accommodation until you get there.

You have to move quickly, too. Although the web is
excellent at conveying up-to-the-second information, last-
minute deals can go very quickly – sometimes even while

you're browsing the site! So if you spot something that takes your fancy, leap at it straight away. There's nothing more annoying than making up your mind to be impulsive only to find that there are no seats left of the plane you want to travel on. Also, the usual condition attached to this kind of special offer is that you don't get a refund if you cancel.

Many of the holiday sites already mentioned above also include 'last-minute' and 'late-availability' offers on their sites. In fact, you may begin to suspect that holiday companies and travel agents use these tags as a bit of a marketing gimmick, knowing what suckers we are for a bargain. Occasionally the 'last-minute' prices on some flights and holidays don't look too different from those with departure dates that are months away.

As ever, it pays to be wary and shop around. The sites listed below

TIP

Make sure you have a rough idea about the usual of cost of the holiday to help you decide whether or not you are really bagging a bargain before committing yourself.

make a feature of offering this kind of discounted deal.

Lastminute.com (www.lastminute.com)
So much attention is lavished on this company's stock market performance and the personalities of its founders that you can easily forget that it's a very good website. Lastminute has been assiduously doing deals with airlines, hotel chains, and holiday companies in its bid to become Europe's premier bargain holiday site. It's fair to say that Lastminute caters to those people looking for a more exotic break than a lost weekend in Ibiza. The search engine is dynamic and responsive to your answers in a way that shows you how customer-focused Lastminute is.

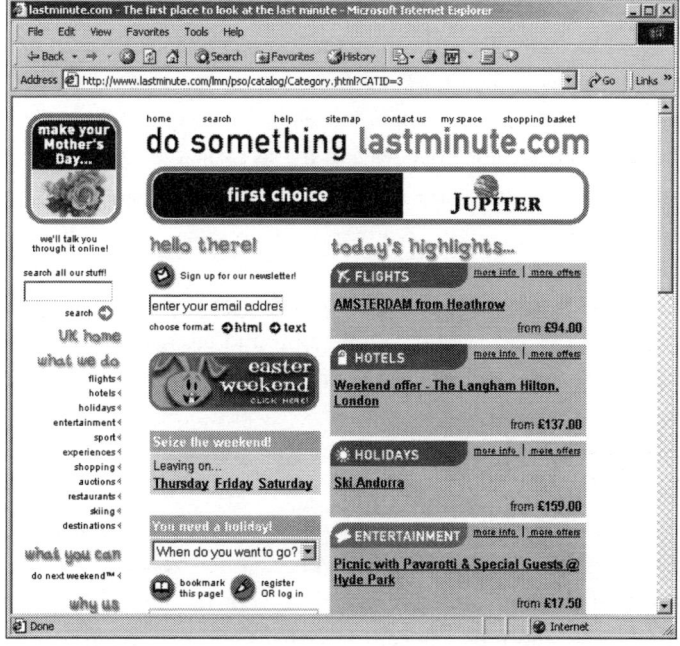

This much-hyped website remains a leading player in doing just what its name suggests – offering last minute discounted holidays and flights (www.lastminute.com).

Bargainholidays (www.bargainholidays.com)

Bargainholidays has quickly established itself as one of the leading package holiday aggregator services, with over 70,000 package holiday deals to choose from, as well as a wealth of resort and weather information to help you plan your holiday. The site concentrates mostly on package deals to the Balearics, as do most of the last-minute specialists. If you're looking for a more do-it-yourself approach and a wider choice of destinations, you're probably better off looking elsewhere.

Travelchoice (www.travelchoice.co.uk)

This is the one of the travel agents owned by First Choice. It selects some of the best last-minute holiday bargains offered by the major tour operators. The site is nice and simple and there's a section for holidays and flights available 'this weekend'. The emphasis is on typical package holiday destinations.

Go-nowtravel.com (www.go-nowtravel.com)

Although this is a well-organised all-round internet travel agent, it is most notable for its offer of over one million late-availability deals on its database. You can browse the list according to your favourite tour operator, or simply by what's available for the coming weekend. You can sort the results of your search in a number of ways – by price, for example – but booking is by phone only. You can click on a 'Phone me' button, type in your phone number and one of the reps will call you. That's good customer service.

Global Travel (www.globalholidays.co.uk)

This Leeds-based independent travel agent has agreements with over 300 tour operators and claims to offer some of the lowest prices on last-minute holidays, short breaks and flights in the UK. You can subscribe to an e-mail newsletter that informs of the latest deals. Booking is by phone.

Late Deals (www.latedeals.co.uk)

Late Deals is part of the Thomson travel group and concentrates on package deals to the main tourist destinations. It organises the holidays according to the proximity of the departure date and whether they are self-catering or all-inclusive.

Holidays in Britain

Visit Britain (www.visitbritain.com)
See page 29.

About Britain (www.aboutbritain.com)
See page 29.

Walking Britain (www.walkingbritain.co.uk)
As you might expect, there's everything the walking
enthusiast could want from a website, including routes,
planners, accommodation suggestions and mouthwatering
photographs to inspire you. You can either sort out your
own holiday or go through one of the several walking tour
operators featured on the site. If you really want to appreciate

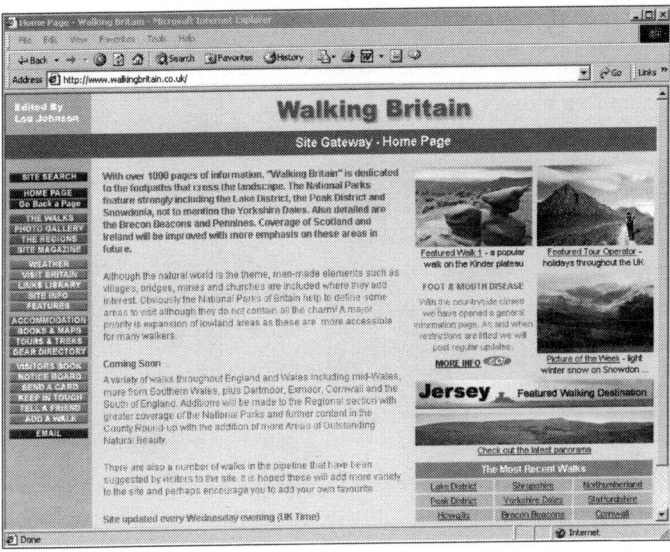

*Walking enthusiasts couldn't ask for more from this comprehensive guide to
walking tours in Britain, ranging from package deals to suggested
independent routes (www.walkingbritain.co.uk).*

the best that the British countryside has to offer, then a walking holiday is a must. You can also order books and maps online.

Britain Express (www.britainexpress.com)
A handy directory of UK tour operators for all the holidays in Britain you can shake a stick at. Also includes guides to these fair isles.

Skiing holidays

Skiing requires a section all of its own, primarily because it is so popular – around a million people in this country actually seem to like it – and because there are so many ski-related websites dedicated to bringing pistes to all mankind. Luckily we don't attempt to name them all here, but we do select some of the leading contenders in a rapidly expanding market.

> **TIP**
>
> Specialist operators tend to be more flexible than standard holiday companies, allowing you to mix and match your requirements as a way of reducing the overall price.

By all accounts, skiing is a complicated business. There's all the equipment and clothing to worry about, the quality of the snow, the weather, avalanches, not to mention the accommodation and getting there in the first place. That's a lot of variables to consider, so ski sites tend to be jam-packed with information – more verbiage than Verbier, as it were.

Thankfully, the web is very good at handling large quantities of data, so booking ski holidays online has become a lot easier and cheaper, giving skiers more control over the various elements of the trip. Some websites allow you to mix and match your requirements, choosing a lower standard of accommodation, for example, as a way of reducing the overall price. Specialist operators can be more flexible this way compared to standard all-round holiday companies.

Here are some of the best ski holiday websites:

1Ski (www.1ski.com)

Publishing giant EMAP produces this excellent and comprehensive ski site. It offers over 200,000 holidays on its database, all searchable on a number of criteria. You can find out the latest snow news and weather reports, even viewing live pictures of resorts thanks to hundreds of web cams streaming images to the site. There are plenty of resort guides, tips and general advice, plus a bulletin board for skiers to swap tales of black runs and après-ski. You can even buy your ski equipment online if you're serious about the sport, and purchase travel insurance. In short, there's everything for every skier, from the novice to the downhill demon.

Ski Holidays (www.ski-holidays.com)

Ski Holidays claims to offer the 'biggest choice of ski deals on the net' from over 100 tour operators. Booking is done by phone and there are the usual last-minute special deals for the impulsive skier.

IfYouSki (www.ifyouski.com)

This site was formerly called Complete Skier and was founded by former British Olympic Ski Team member Michael Liebreich. There are plenty of package holidays on offer plus special deals, and the ability to book accommodation only. There's a thriving community of skiing enthusiasts to share views and experiences with and a regular e-mail newsletter to sign up to. Booking is by telephone.

1 Ski (top, www.1ski.com) is possibly the best skiing holiday website on the internet, catering for beginners and experts alike with holidays, equipment, insurance and weather reports. Another skiing website, Iglu (bottom, www.iglu.com) places the emphasis on ski accommodation, but includes links to tour operators offering package skiing holidays.

Iglu (www.iglu.com)

Iglu specialises in finding a wide range of accommodation in each resort, providing detailed listings of the property features. It has extended its accommodation coverage to summer villas also. There are lots of ski holidays from the leading tour operators and all the usual ski information, from interactive maps to web cams at the resorts. Iglu guarantees to match the price of any other travel company offering exactly the same holiday.

Rocket Ski (www.rocketski.com)

This skiing and snowboarding site prides itself on its flexibility. You can book each element of the holiday separately or combine them. With a site like this, you know that the people running it actually know their stuff. Worth a serious look for ski freaks. You can also book online.

The Ski Club of Great Britain (www.skiclub.co.uk)

This website is replete with news and snow reports. Members qualify for discounts on holidays and insurance.

Ski Esprit (www.ski-esprit.co.uk)

Despite the image of skiing as an activity exclusive to 'bright young things' with more money than sense, plenty of families enjoy it too. Ski Esprit tailors its service entirely towards children, providing childcare, skiing tuition and plenty of other activities for kids, leaving time for parents to escape. In a similar vein, the eponymous **Family Ski Company** (www.familyski.co.uk) is also worth a look.

Other activity holidays

Adventure Directory (www.adventuredirectory.com)

For specialist adventure holidays – the ones that usually involve risk to life and limb, and which often are not covered by standard travel insurance policies – try the Adventure Directory. It lists hundreds of operators who specialise in over 40 adventure activities, from base jumping to white-water rafting. Just interrogate the database and choose your ideal holiday destination. The site also includes lots of guides, tips and features for the budding adrenaline-junkie.

Travel with Bicycles (www.bikeaccess.net/default.cfm)

Ever considered taking your bike on holiday? As well as tips on how to pack it, comparing the cost and handling habits of

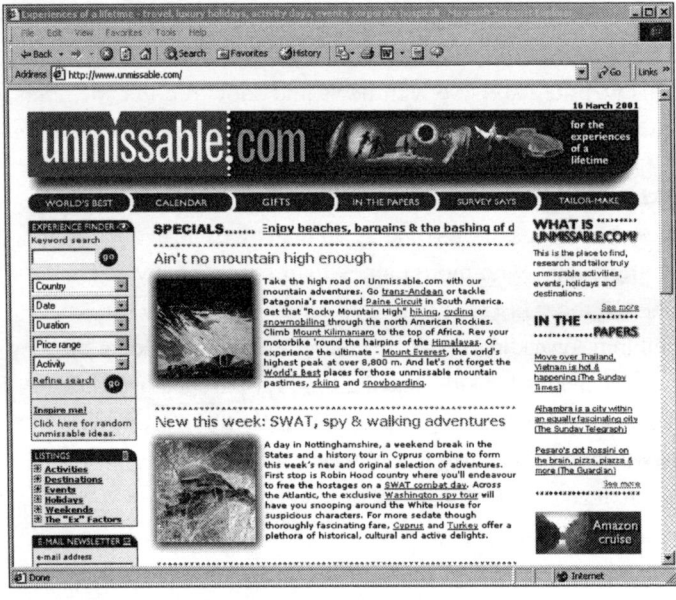

If you're looking for a holiday with a little glamour or adventure, away from the crowds, Unmissable (www.unmissable.com) has the answer – but it's not for the budget traveller.

various airlines, railway and bus companies, the site provides bicycle route information from airports to major cities. There's information on hiring bikes around the world, and plenty of ideas on where to go and what to do on two wheels.

Unmissable (www.unmissable.com)

For those fed up with the same old holiday year in year out, this site should give some interesting alternatives. If you're happy to splash out a bit in return for something truly memorable, Unmissable offers a mouthwatering range of speciality holidays. For example, you could explore the world's fast-dwindling rainforests in Borneo, or take the Orient Express to Venice. As well as long-stay holidays, Unmissable offers themed breaks and activities, such as hiring a luxury sports car for a weekend's driving in the country while staying in a top-class hotel. If you have the money, Unmissable will certainly help you spend it.

Travelchest (www.travelchest.co.uk)

Travelchest caters for 'the more discerning traveller', which usually translates as 'the wealthier traveller'. If you want complete control over the type of holiday you have, from the destination to the accommodation and travel arrangements, Travelchest will arrange it for you. The site is stylishly designed using Flash animation software, so make sure you have a Flash reader installed.

Voyages Jules Verne (www.vjv.co.uk)

None of your package holidays to Ibiza on this site. These are holidays for this 'discerning traveller' we keep hearing about, as the website makes clear. Whether you fancy exploring the Amazon Basin or touring the world-famous appellations of Bordeaux, VJV can offer an exotic themed holiday for you. Don't expect bargain basement prices, just holidays to remember.

Cruises

Just like skiing, cruises are a whole holiday sub-category on their own. There are so many options available and so many operators specialising in them that aggregator websites make sense for most people, unless you insist on sailing on the *QE2*, of course.

Ecruise (www.ecruise.co.uk)

If you're new to the whole idea of cruises this site will point you in the right direction. It collates and categorises cruises from a large range of operators and includes over 600 cut-price and late-availability cruises.

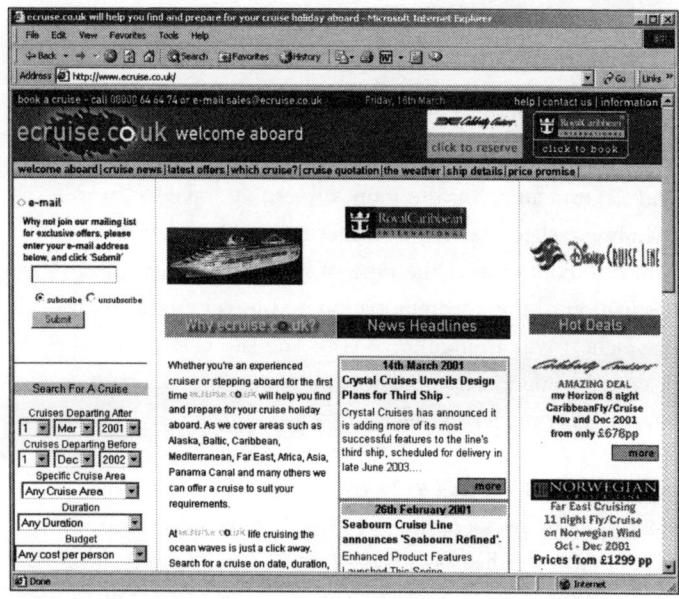

Every type of cruise can be found on the Ecruise website (www.ecruise. co.uk), from luxury to tourist class, as well as practical advice for novice seafarers.

Cunard Line (www.cunardlines.co.uk)

When only the best will do, sail on the *QE2* . . . or the *Caronia*.

Cruise (www.cruise.com)

This US discount cruise agent, owned by Omega World Travel, claims to be the internet's largest. It promises to reduce the cruise lines' lowest prices by 5% to 10% the first time you book.

Holiday auctions

We looked at how online auctions work in **Flight auctions** (*see page 55*) But if you've made a beeline straight for this chapter, then here's a recap. Online auctions work in much the same way as conventional auctions. You find something you want to bid for and you bid against others who are also interested. The big difference is that you don't have to be in the auction room to take part. Indeed, bidders can be thousands of miles apart thanks to the interactive capabilities of the web.

First, you register with an online auction site so that it can identify you properly when you make a bid. This process usually involves you giving your credit card details as well.

General auction sites have many categories of items up for auction, from memorabilia to holidays. If something appeals, you can place a bid. Bids generally go up in set increments, and you can often set the system to increase your bids automatically up to your cut-off price. This means you don't have to stay chained to your screen, watching to see if you've been outbid.

Each lot will have accompanying information telling you when the auction will close. The later you leave it, the less chance there is of being outbid. One thing to bear in mind is that there will often be a reserve price placed on the auction item. This is the minimum price the vendor is willing to accept. Auctions will usually say whether the reserve has been met, but you don't often know what that reserve is.

The other main type of auction is the reverse auction. Instead of competing against other bidders, you indicate the price you are willing to pay for a holiday and then wait to discover whether any tour operator will take you up on your offer. The idea originated in the USA, but is starting to attract interest over here, too.

Before you commit yourself to any auction bidding process, check out the conditions. You may find that you can't travel at a convenient time, or you may have to stay a certain number of nights. Also make sure that you have a good idea what the holiday is worth before you start bidding. It would be pointless to bid too much when the main idea of an auction is that you save money.

WARNING

Before you commit yourself to any auction bidding process, check out the conditions.

Similarly with reverse auctions. You have to have a reasonable idea of the value of the holiday you're making an offer for. Pitch too low and you're not likely to find any takers. Pitch too high and you could end up paying more than you would via a conventional holiday website.

QXL Ricardo (www.qxl.com/uk)

QXL is Europe's leading online auction site. Its 'Travel Shop' section contains various categories of holiday that are up for auction, from city breaks to African safaris. QXL lets you know whether the vendor is a private person or a merchant partner. In the case of holidays, they're almost exclusively from tour operators.

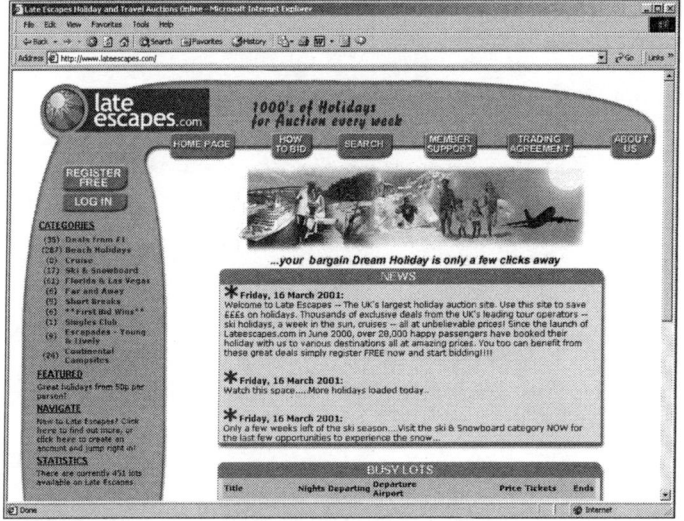

If your destination and departure requirements are flexible, buying a holiday by auction can be a very economic solution – Late Escapes (www.lateescapes.com) is one of the largest holiday auction sites.

Late Escapes (www.lateescapes.com)

This auction site, launched in June 2000 by the holiday operator Airtours, claims to be the UK's largest holiday auction site. More than 18,000 holidaymakers had won bids for holidays since launch when I checked out the site, and there were 367 lots available. The bidding on some featured holidays can start as low as 50p per person.

Internet Travel Auctions (www.holidayauctions.net)

This site gives you the choice of auctions and standard late-availability deals. The range isn't massive, but there were still some interesting potential bargains to be snapped up when I looked.

Chapter 7

Travel Insurance and Foreign Currency

Travel insurance

There's plenty of research to show that we've been paying through the nose for our travel insurance, largely because we buy it from the travel agent at the time we book the holiday. Compared to the amount we're paying for the holiday itself, the insurance cost seems puny. But when insurance is bundled in with a holiday we can end up paying more than double the amount we would pay if we bought a policy separately. In fact, one insurer has estimated that travel agent commission can be as high as 70% on some policies.

Fortunately, the low distribution cost of the internet and its ability to compare prices is helping to rectify the situation. So next time you remember to buy travel insurance, don't be pushed into buying a policy on the spot by a travel agent, get online and start doing some proper research. You may be surprised at the savings you could make.

Although the web is excellent at comparing quotes, be careful that products are being compared on a like-for-like basis. The premium may be the most competitive but only because the level of cover is inferior, or the excess is huge.

For example, if you're booking a skiing holiday, don't assume your standard travel insurance policy covers winter sports activities – it often won't. You may be able to pay a top-up, but check also which types of activity are covered. For example, off-piste skiing is often excluded altogether.

And don't forget to check whether your credit, charge or gold card comes with any free travel insurance. You may not have to pay for a new policy at all if you're lucky. But be careful to read the smallprint for exclusions and so on.

When scouting around for a cheap policy, have a look at a number of sources. Most of the travel websites have links to insurers. Try these out but don't rely on them. Have a look at some of the personal finance information sites as well. These contain a wealth of information, from general guides, to 'best buy' tables and links to insurers.

WARNING

Don't assume that online travel insurance quotes will always be the cheapest.

Also try online insurance brokers that do a lot of the shopping around for you. Lastly, because you can't assume that the broker will cover the whole market, check out a few direct insurers as well. Unfortunately, you can't assume that online travel insurance quotes will always be the cheapest. Telephone brokers can still come up trumps every now and then.

Here's a selection of websites to get you started:

Personal finance information sites

FTYourMoney	**www.ftyourmoney.com**
Moneyextra	**www.moneyextra-insurance.com**
FIND (directory)	**www.find.co.uk**

Insurers and brokers

All the following sites offer the option to buy online:

Barclays Bank	www.barclays.co.uk
CGU Direct	www.cgu-direct.co.uk
Columbus Direct	www.columbusdirect.co.uk
Direct Line	www.directline.com
Eagle Star Direct	www.eaglestar.co.uk
Egg	www.egg.com
Endsleigh	www.endsleigh.co.uk
Halifax	www.halifax.co.uk
Norwich Union Direct	www.norwich-union.co.uk/products/insurance/travel
Preferential	www.preferential.co.uk
Rapidinsure	www.rapidinsure.co.uk
Screentrade	www.screentrade.co.uk
STA Travel	www.sta-travel.com
The RAC	www.rac.co.uk
Trailfinders	www.trailfinders.co.uk
Travel-Insurance Direct	www.travel-insurance.net
Worldtraveldirect	www.worldtraveldirect.com

The Association of British Insurers (www.abi.org.uk)

The insurance industry's main trade association has produced a free leaflet explaining the ins and outs of holiday insurance and advice on motoring abroad. To read the leaflet you need to have Adobe Acrobat Reader loaded on your computer. If you don't, you can download it from the Adobe website (www.adobe.com) or install it from one of the CD-ROMs that often accompany computer and internet magazines. It is a very common program and well worth having as it is rapidly becoming the standard format for many online documents.

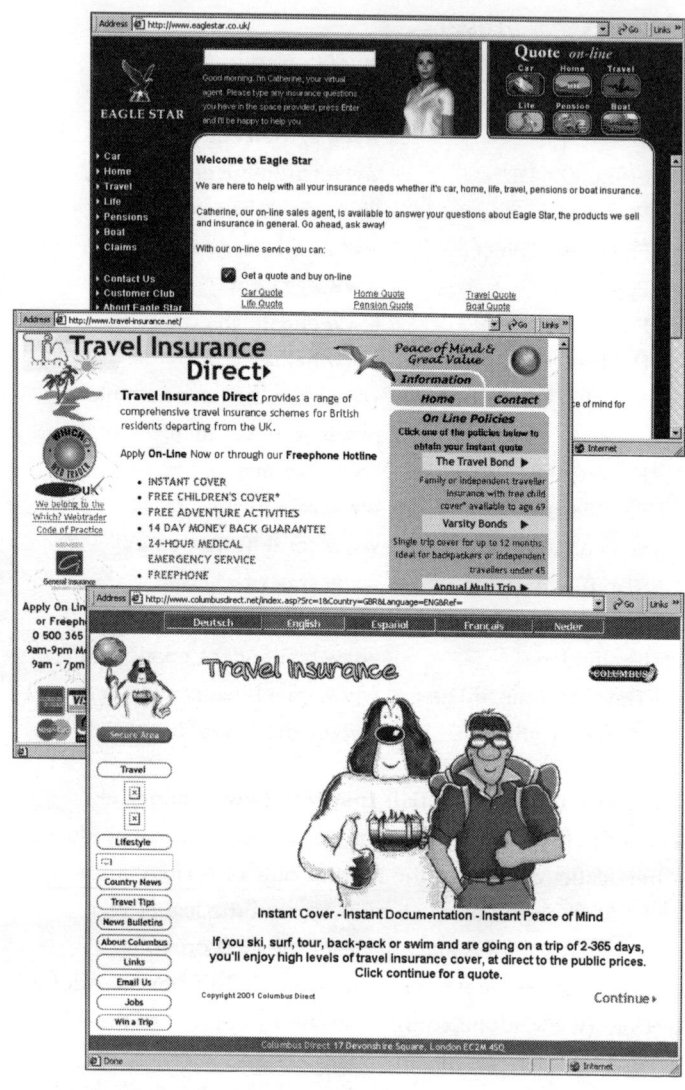

Numerous companies now offer travel insurance online, from general insurance brokers such as Eagle Star (top, www.eaglestar.co.uk), to those companies specialising in travel, such as Travel-Insurance Direct (centre, www.travel-insurance.net) and Columbus Direct (bottom, www.columbusdirect.co.uk).

Foreign currency

Buying foreign currency and traveller's cheques is usually the last thing on our minds when organising a trip or holiday. We often leave it to the last minute and end up being fleeced with poor exchange rates at airport bureaux de change. These days the need to take cash or TCs with us is far less pressing thanks to the growing network of cash machines around the world and the extension of international network agreements between card companies.

But if you like the security of cash in your back pocket (sensible if the only cash machine in the mountain village doesn't work) then the web can help you order your currency quickly and efficiently. Why waste time queuing in a bank or post office when you can have it delivered for a small fee?

Below we give you some online foreign currency vendors to look at. Be sure to compare exchange rates and delivery charges before flashing the plastic.

> **TIP**
>
> *Be sure to compare exchange rates and delivery charges before buying foreign currency online.*

Thomas Cook (www.thomascook.co.uk)

UK travel agent Thomas Cook offers a very easy-to-use foreign currency and traveller's cheques ordering service. There's no commission to pay, just a £5 delivery charge. Be careful though – the quoted exchange rate is unlikely to be the most competitive you can find. But for those in a hurry and with important things to worry about – like getting to the airport in time – a few pounds here and there won't matter. You buy online using a credit or debit card over a secure encrypted link.

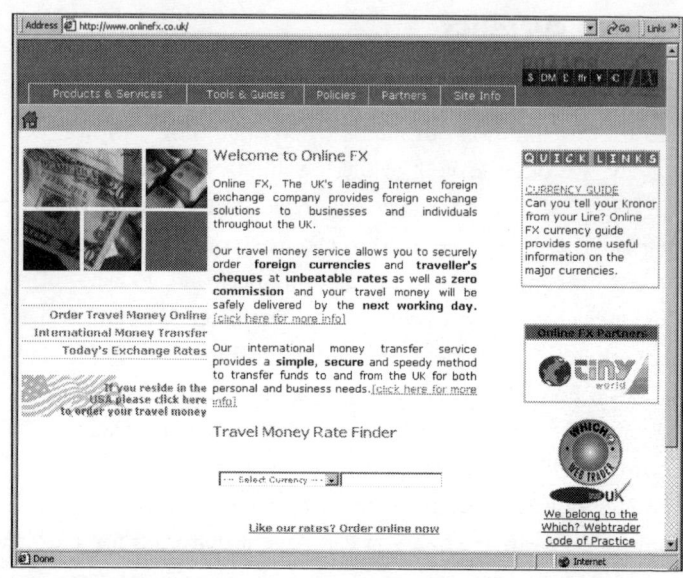

OnlineFX (www.onlinefx.co.uk) is one of many companies now offering foreign currency via the internet, but benefits particularly from its lack of commission charges and guaranteed next-day delivery.

OnlineFX (www.onlinefx.co.uk)

Online FX offers much the same type of service as Thomas Cook, with most of the world's major currencies included. Delivery is next day guaranteed and there's no commission. Online FX will also buy excess currency back from you at the end of your trip. When I compared French Franc rates, Online FX came out significantly better. Delivery, at £3.95, was also cheaper.

Dollars

SimplyFX (www.simplyfx.com)   In Receivership!

A very simply designed service notable for the lack of commission or delivery charges. The price you see on-screen is the price you get. The only potential drawback is that delivery is within three days, not by the next day. If you're happy to wait you could save yourself a few pounds.

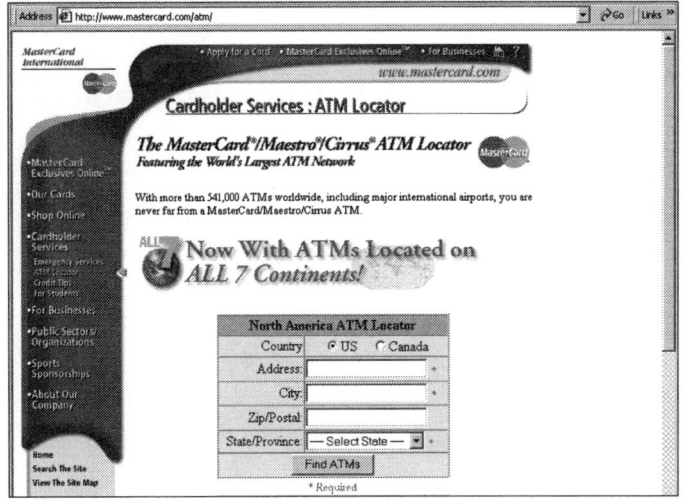

The major credit cards, such as Mastercard (www.mastercard.com/atm), now have useful websites detailing the locations of their automatic teller machines all over the world.

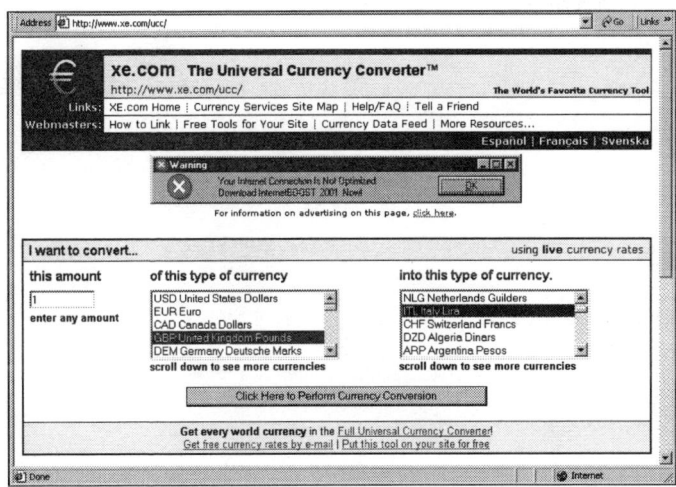

Finding out up-to-the-minute rates of exchange couldn't be easier – at the Universal Currency Converter (www.xe.com/ucc) simply type in the currencies and amount you want to convert and the answer appears on the screen.

ATM locations

Visa	www.visa.com/pd/atm
Mastercard	www.mastercard.com/atm

Currency converters

Many of the general holiday websites include currency converters, but here are a couple of other addresses for your bookmarks list:

Yahoo!	http://quote.yahoo.com/m3?u
Universal Currency Converter	www.xe.com/ucc

Chapter 8

Your Rights

Introduction

Just because you book travel and holidays over the web doesn't mean that you're not protected under the law, just as if you'd booked through a travel agent or direct from a holiday company or airline. But you do have to apply some common sense and basic rules before committing any money.

Most online holiday companies are members of trade associations that give consumers protection if things go wrong. We give you the relevant addresses below and some addresses of passenger organisations you can complain to if you're unhappy with any aspect of travel. Lastly, there are some general safe surfing tips to keep you out of the clutches of unscrupulous online operators.

The Association of British Travel Agents
(www.abtanet.com)
Make sure that any travel agent website you come across is a member of ABTA. An ABTA-bonded agent is obliged to refund your money if the holiday company goes bust before

The ABTA website (www.abtanet.com) will inform you whether your travel company is an ABTA member – which ensures compensation if the holiday goes wrong.

Similar to ABTA, a travel company's ATOL membership protects their customers if an airline should go bust. The website www.atol.org.uk offers all the necessary information on member companies and claim forms.

you go. You're also guaranteed not to be left high and dry if things go pear-shaped while you're actually on holiday.

ABTA has 600 tour operator members and over 2,300 travel agents responsible for selling around 90% of all UK package holidays. ABTA also operates an independent arbitration scheme should you have reason to complain about one of its members. Check out its website for the rules and contact details.

Air Travel Organiser's Licensing (ATOL)
(www.atol.org.uk)

This scheme is managed by the Civil Aviation Authority and protects consumers from losing money or being stranded abroad if air travel companies go bust. If the travel website offers flights or international package tours, make sure it is a member of ATOL as well as ABTA. Look for the logos on the website. The ATOL site also includes claim forms, factsheets, and detailed advice for holidaymakers who find themselves up the creek. Check its database to see if a company you're dealing with is actually a member of the scheme.

Association of Independent Tour Operators (AITO)
(www.aito.co.uk)

Although this association doesn't provide any financial protection for holidaymakers, it does at least insist on its members adhering to a code of practice that forbids inaccurate brochures, for example.

International Air Transport Association (www.iata.org)

IATA is another abbreviation to watch out for on travel websites. It is the main association for the airline industry, providing information to travellers about airlines and how they operate. But it doesn't have any compliance function and won't intervene if you have a dispute with an airline.

IATA is the place to go if you want to find out anything about an airline. You can also check the website (www.iata.org) to see if the airline you are flying is a member.

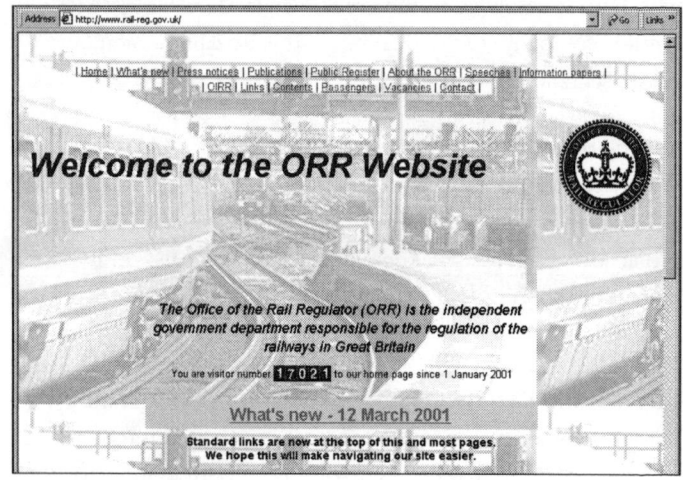

Everything you need to know about the current running of Britain's rail network should be found on the government's rail regulator website (www.rail-reg.gov.uk)

Regulators and passenger organisations

Civil Aviation Authority	**www.caa.co.uk**
Office of the Rail Regulator	**www.rail-reg.gov.uk**
Rail Passengers Council	**http://www.rail-reg.gov.uk/ rucc/rucindex.htm**
Department of Transport	**www.detr.gov.uk**
EmbassyWeb	**www.embassyweb.com**

Safe surfing

The most important safety tip when booking travel services and holidays online is never to give your credit card details – or any other personal details for that matter – over an insecure internet link. Encryption of sensitive data is now standard, making online transactions very safe. There's no excuse for serious websites not to offer total security. You can tell if a website offers a secure link in the following ways:

1. your web browser will show a security symbol, such as a closed padlock, at the bottom of the screen

2. the web address may change to begin **https://** rather than the usual **http://**.

Encrypting data takes a lot of computer resources and can slow things down considerably on the web, so what many online retailers do is give you the option of switching between secure and insecure mode. If you're just browsing the site there's no reason for the link to be secure – you're not transmitting any sensitive information. But if you proceed to the booking stage, the link should switch to a secure one. If it doesn't, don't go any further until you've clarified the situation with the website.

If you've never heard of the company whose website you've come across, how do you know it is genuine and reliable? How do you know that it will keep your credit card details secure from theft, internal or external? In short, you don't. You have to satisfy yourself about genuineness and reliability, although there are a number of accreditation schemes around, such as *Which?* WebTrader, to lend authority to genuine websites.

Follow these rules if you're unsure about a site:

1. Never give your card details over the net except via a secure server.

2. Never write down or disclose passwords, log-in names or Personal Identification Numbers (PINs).

3. Stick to well-known, well-regarded websites if possible. Ask friends for recommendations.

4. Look for a physical address and telephone contact numbers. Test them to establish that the business really exists. Ask your friends if they've heard of it. If you have any remaining doubts, don't deal with them.

5. Also check that the web address is exactly right. Fraudsters can sometimes set up virtual copies of well-known brand-name websites. A dot here and a hyphen there can make all the difference. And bear in mind that a .co.uk or .uk ending doesn't necessarily mean that the site is based in the UK.

6. Look for sites that have been given a 'kitemark' certificate by an accreditation scheme, such as VeriSign, *Which?* WebTrader from the Consumers' Association, or TrustUK. Such schemes check out websites for authenticity, security, and responsibility in the handling of personal details.

⑦ Look for sites that send you e-mail confirmation of bookings.

⑧ Make sure the travel site is a member of the relevant trade associations (*see page 125*).

⑨ If you're dealing with a financial product provider, for example when buying travel insurance, check that it is fully authorised for its range of activities. You can check the company against the Financial Services Authority's central register (**www.thecentralregister.co.uk**).

⑩ If a website is offering deals that look too good to be true, you might want to question how long it's likely to stay in business. The travel industry is particularly competitive and cut-throat. Although you're not likely to lose any money if a company goes bust, most of us would prefer to avoid such hassle if possible.

⑪ Use a credit card to pay online. The card issuer is obliged to refund you under Section 75 of the Consumer Credit Act if things go wrong.

Index